HOPE AGAINST HOPE

WALTER HOLTON CAPPS

HOPE
AGAINST HOPE

MOLTON TO MERTON IN ONE DECADE

Fortress Press
Philadelphia

Library of Congress Catalog Card Number 75-36456

ISBN 0-8006-0436-9

5412K75   Printed in the United States of America   1-436

for Solveig and Milton Grimsrud
whose daughter is my best friend
whose rootedness enriches openness

CONTENTS

Preface   ix

PART ONE: PROFILES   1

   1. The Advent of the Protean Style   3

   2. The Recovery of the Body   18

   3. What Ever Happened to Hope?   33

PART TWO: PROVISIONS   49

   4. The Dynamics of Positive Disengagement   51

   5. Wisdom from the Analytical Fathers   75

PART THREE: PROJECTIONS   103

   6. The Return of Homo Eremeticus   105

   7. Hope's Revised Charter   130

   8. Moltmann and Merton   147

PREFACE

"What do you think of Karl Barth?" was the first question asked of me when I arrived to teach in the newly established department of religious studies in the University of California, Santa Barbara, in the fall of 1964. It was an appropriate question, though it made me curious when it was put to me in that place at that time. I learned later that my colleague, W. Richard Comstock, had been greeted with "what do you think of Paul Tillich?" when he had come to the same campus the year before. This too was an appropriate question, though it made him curious when it was put to him in that place at that time. In either form the question was the same. In those days, persons whose orientation to religion had been formed by the theology of the Protestant seminaries seemed to be Barthian, more or less, or Tillichian, more or less. The major lines of controversy were formed by the differences between the two points of departure. Thus, spotting Barthians and Tillichians was almost like identifying Republicans and Democrats: it provided reliable indices into characteristic allegiances, deepest interests, typical awarenesses, and notable biases. And the differences were even to become perceptible in approaches taken to the academic study of religion on the state university campus.[1]

This was the situation ten years ago, when the Christian world was preoccupied with the matter of its own openness to contemporary cultural experience. Understandably,

Barth and Tillich were seen as the two most eloquent spokes-men for the two most representative and self-consistent positions. The former tended to favor a narrowing of what counted as authentic religion while the latter gave expres-sion to a greater elasticity.

What reciprocity is there between the uniqueness of the Christian faith and the ways of the modern world? It is the perennial question. Barth and Tillich had become the new-est champions of two prominent contrasting attitudes toward religion in the west. The same attitudes had had able representation at the time of the Enlightenment too, for example, when the question was posed in terms of the relation of revealed to natural religion. The same attitudes had been sustained in the more recent wrestling of Chris-tians with the force of secularization. The updated, twen-tieth-century formulation evinced the same question: Is the strength of the Christian faith to be found in a disposition which can be harmonized with the tendency of the modern world? Is contemporary cultural experience acceptable to the Christian faith, or must it first be refined, purged, or significantly complemented? Is the world primarily an audience, a receptor, a receiver of the revealed message, or does it contribute reliable content? Or is the world an adversary, provoking an inevitable contest? In each ver-sion the question is the same. And its expression is not restricted to Protestant thought, for Catholic theology too—witness the interests of Rahner, Küng, Suenens, Schille-beeckx, the documents of Vatican Council II—was preoccu-pied with the relation of revealed religious truth to natural and cultural religious experience. The prominence of the question in all parts of the Christian world reflected an enor-mous and intense interest in the encounter between sacred tradition and the modern world. Wherever the interest surfaced, it forced a reassessment of the issue of sanctionability and legitimization.

Much has happened in the ten years intervening. The Christian world has found itself in a state of profound and shocking transition, a veritable revolution. Religious attitudes have been affected. Patterns of belief have been reconstituted. Motivations for action have been reconceived. Conceptions of reality have been redesigned. Religious self-consciousness, in individual and corporate as well as personal and institutional terms, has been experienced and interpreted according to new canons. In all of these dimensions there has been a decided shift to a dynamic, innovative, fluid and mobile, almost experimental orientation. In the process, theologies of change have come to replace theologies of permanence. In the exchange, tradition itself has become more pliable and pluralized: not one sanctionable tradition any longer, but several traditions, of greater and lesser resourcefulness, insightfulness, and contemporary applicability. Throughout the Christian world the intent is to cope with an age in comprehensive transition. And the shifts in attitude and perception have been dramatic, swift, sweeping, deep, and penetrating. There has been a revolution in Christian religious awareness.

The accounts of the transition are so well known that they hardly need to be rehearsed. Typically, they begin with Dietrich Bonhoeffer's World War II musings, meditations, suggestions, or provocative and troublesome prophesies as he faced death in a German prison. Especially significant are his twin declarations: first, the world has come of age, and, second, the time is coming when persons will find it impossible to be religious. The two announcements were intended to be nearly synonymous. Coming of age was to be translated into inability to be religious. Or, seen from the other side, previous traditional religiousness was understood to be a deterrent to the process of human maturation. And yet the deeper power of Bonhoeffer's insight lies in its being proposed as an analysis of western culture. It was offered as an interpretation of the fundamental reverberations in the modern, western world. As Bonhoeffer perceived it, the west was involved in a highly significant transitional phase, a stage in its development which could be likened to the movement from embryonic to post-embryonic in the human life cycle. Its nearer maturity would require that all vestiges of the embryonic state be discarded in favor of dispositions which would keep pace with its subsequent development. The religion of the future could not be like the religion of the past or the present, not if indeed, at long last, the world was coming of age.

Because they stimulated a new set of theological issues, Bonhoeffer's insights turned out to be the fresh currents which overcame the domination of the Barthian-Tillichian contrast. Though precociously instructive, Bonhoeffer's proposals were also somewhat tentative. He displayed both reticence and lack of specificity in making his proclamations and pronouncements. His hints in *Letters and Papers from Prison* were teasers.[2] But, before long the same propositions found impressive articulation in Harvey Cox's discovery and celebration of "the secular city."[3] The previous juxtaposition of sacred and modern—a little of this, a little of that, or all of this and none of that—was upstaged by the contention that the modern world, with all of its diversity and complexity, could be perceived as being sacred. The modern world need not be conceived as being anti- or extra-sacred, for the modern, as modern, is sanctionable. Almost in one fell swoop, secularity was made the occasion for religious celebration.

We pursued the new current to its ultimate conclusions, drawing as much as we could upon the here-and-now world, relying as much as we could upon its resources, devoted as much as we could to specificity, worshipping concreteness, committed to the full to what Michael Novak called "the unfeigned love of this earth and of the concrete singular."[4] It was understandable that some found it both possible and necessary to proceed further, to celebrate "the death of God" for religious reasons. It was appropriate that the transcendental "other-worldly" God should die, and it was understandable that Dietrich Bonhoeffer's name should be invoked as an advocate of the God-is-dead theology. The purging of transcendence was just as implicit in Bonhoeffer's inveighings against "the god beyond the borders" as it was in Nietzsche's nihilism. The diminishing of transcendence can be taken in two ways: one can stress the utter absence of God from human affairs or one can emphasize the contrasting presence of God in exclusively human, this-worldly form. Thus, the unmasking of transcendence can be utilized to support an incarnational emphasis or it can be seen as an exorcism of stultifying mystification. It can be regarded as its own reward or as the occasion for something else.

Thus, secularity extended made immanence normative. And the new theology of hope, born in 1965, only carried the immanentist dictate further when it concentrated on the coming of the Kingdom of God in realistic, religio-secularist terms. For by now the ideal commonwealth was no longer an ephemeral gleam or a pious wish, but an actual possibility in very specific and concrete socio-political terms. Bonhoeffer's prison prophesies about "the world's coming of age" found concrete embodiment in the contentions of the theology of hope. To paraphrase Whitehead's comment about Plato and his influence upon early Christianity: what Bonhoeffer divined in theory, Cox proclaimed in fact. And, we must add, what Cox proclaimed and celebrated, Jürgen Moltmann specified and embellished on a more conscious, deliberate, biblical base. Then, prompted by additional firsthand experience, sharper perceptions, and more acute sensitivities to the deep agonies of the secular city, especially in those settings where oppression and alienation are most blatantly pronounced, the theology of hope gave wings to a theology of liberation, whose currents, at last reckoning, had not yet run dry.

Just as Bonhoeffer had foretold, it was a curious, fascinating, topsy-turvy situation. Western culture was experiencing a significant transition of extraordinary religious consequence. Its coming of age was related to loss of traditional patterns of religious belief. Yet, in the process, many persons discovered that personal religious sensitivity could be sustained, though with a radically revised self-understanding because its conceptual moorings had been transformed. What was possible formerly only on transcendent grounds also became accessible, though in different terms, on an immanentist basis. The relinquishment of a firm hold on permanence, for example, didn't destroy personal enthusiasms. The shift from other-worldliness to this-worldliness didn't seem to qualify confidence in one's salvation. Identifying redemption with the realization of the Kingdom of God didn't diminish individual interest or involvement. The massive shift in attitude and perspective, in short, didn't lessen religious vitality, but, instead, only seemed to instill a new verve. Even after the supporting conceptual framework had been dramatically overhauled, faith seemed sustainable, though on a basis contrary to the former outlook.

But the changes that came did not occur in straight-line

forward fashion. It was not as though there was but one strong, compelling current which moved with force, dignity, resoluteness, and without resistance toward achieving its goals. The transition was more ambiguous. For, along the way, the counter theme gathered momentum. With the movement away from transcendence to immanence came a renewed interest in recovering transcendence. Concomitant with the identification of the sacred with the modern came a new, forceful, and radical critique of the secular city. With the conjunction of the sacred and the modern came an updated sense of the propriety of "Christ against culture" motifs. With the interest in establishing the Kingdom of God on earth came a fresh awareness that "my kingdom is not of this world." With the demand that the dictates of the gospel influence society's corporate structure came a fresh wave of openness to mystical experience. By the end of the decade, contrary currents found impressive representation. Change was in full sway, but also in full view. Transformations had been effected, but painfully, not always playfully. Innovations had come about, but through destruction, not facile substitution. After the full force of change had been felt, when fascination also discovered terror, there was a turn toward simplicity and stability even if the possibility of recovering permanence had been foreclosed. Accompanying preoccupation with the "concrete singular" came a renewed dependence upon the interconnectedness of things. And with the interest in doing-something-now-and-doing-it-here came a request for a comprehensive vision in which each thing is given proper place, but not necessarily as an exclusive ordering principle.

Some of us approached the era a decade ago greatly intrigued by the theology of hope, largely because this theology enunciated many of the new themes in a religiously compelling and conceptually integrative manner. This new revised "social gospel" worked to overturn the perspective within which faith was understood primarily in personal terms, and religion referred to the relation of man to God (or to the Ultimate, Infinite, Absolute, Beyond, or, as some had said, to "whatever it is you call it"). In the former orientation, social action was not necessarily fundamental to faith, but was interpreted as an expression, or an outgrowth, of the primary matter. With the institution of the theology of hope, the priorities of faith were redressed: the salvation of the individual depended upon the corporate fate of the human race. But by 1975, just a decade following the publication of Moltmann's *Theology of Hope,*[5] many Christians seemed more comfortable with personal piety again, rather than with social or political involvement. It was topsy-turvy, back and forth, with contrary alternations. The previous traditional emphasis upon transcendent realities (heaven, eternal life, and inwardness) had given way to a fresh concern about things more concrete, this-worldly, and more socially and politically engaging. Then, having established this new concern as something which belonged integrally to religion's and theology's agenda, we watched, somewhat surprised, as the pendulum swung back to recover the religious priorities we had all but abandoned. The previous rather traditional regard for the life of the *spirit* was challenged by the newer recognition of the value of the *body.* Then, having pursued this train for awhile, the pendulum swung back to the former orientation to correct newly discovered excesses. The previous age-old preoccupation with tradition and authority became subservient to a new sensitivity toward innovation and personal creativity; the intent of both was to maximize individual and corporate personal liberty. But, true to form, the newer perceptions were modified by oscillations back to the original point of departure. And so the rhythms seemed to go. From contemplation to action, then from action to contemplation; from spirituality to political theology, then from political theology to spirituality; from inward to outward, then from outward to inward; from permanence to change, then from change to permanence: the alternating transitions were effected within the span of one decade. And during that time we experienced broad, sweeping, almost cyclical alternations in religious orientation. Thus, many of the products of the 1960s and early 1970s—the emphasis on immanence, political action, the world's setting the agenda for the church, etc.—were identified as being dangerous to the faith in the Hartford Appeal of 1975,[6] even by those who had been their most outspoken champions. Still, the social and political dilemmas had not been resolved or satisfactorily clarified. The plight of oppressed peoples had not been significantly corrected. The massive inequities in the very structure of human society had not been altered or redressed. The occasion for a theology of hope—indeed, for a theology of liberation—still remained, in many ways vastly more eloquent and compelling than ever before. At the time of its advent, one had to argue for the propriety of a theology of hope. The issues were primarily conceptual. Now, ten years later, the necessity and rationale were shockingly self-evident. But religious and theological interests were being directed to matters of another dispositional sort. It was a new era. And the conceptual innovations which had provoked and facilitated the transition seem not to have been sustained by the same transition.

What does one make of it? What about the future projected a mere ten years ago? Had it come to pass? Had we been to the future only to find that the future didn't work? Or did the future both work and not work, attract and repel, tantalize and repulse, all at once? Had hope's future been formed by contrariness? Did all that we had set aside return back, hauntingly, teasingly, almost impudently, perhaps to teach us that we had been deceived by oversimplifications, by the expectation of progress via movements straight-line forward? In matters ethical and religious, to paraphrase Kierkegaard, must contrariness always rule? Is the future of religious sensitivity always antinomy? Or was it only loss of nerve?

This is the subject which is treated in the chapters which follow. Both chronicle and probe, our book concentrates on some prominent religious currents and theological fashions which have alternated with each other during the problematic, fascinating, almost cataclysmic decade, beginning in the mid 1960s. It chronicles these currents, then probes the process by which one strain of religious enthusiasms meets then gives way to its opposing counterpart. The book, in short, is about contrariness and its influence in Christian religious imagination.

An earlier work, *Time Invades the Cathedral*,[7] contains the suggestion that there is more than one religion of Christianity, at least two of which are self-consistent. This was not a reference to denominational variety, but, instead, to the large constellations of belief and attitude which function as perspectival bases of Christian self-consciousness regardless of denominational or church sponsorship. The principal suggestion was extended to include the possibility that these several religions may be in tension—perhaps in perpetual tension—with each other. The implication followed that this intrinsic tension may lie at the root of the comprehensive perspectival shifts and transpositions which occur both repeatedly and somewhat predictably in Christian theological reflection, and not least in the contemporary era.

In this book, the earlier suggestion has become a thesis. Tension, or contrariness, has become the subject. And the supporting illustrative materials are some of the prominent religious and theological currents which have prospered during the decade under our scrutiny. The "two-religions-of-Christianity" thesis has found specific application in the contemporary era. For, while the intent to redesign the faith in dynamic, immanentist terms has been revolutionary, it has not become an adequate replacement for the older, more dominant, transcendent orientation. And sometimes it looks as if the immanentist experiment only confirms the dependence of Christian sensibility upon the transcendent vision.

The medium is a series of case studies. Each of the early chapters highlights (or "profiles") a particular example of contrariness in the religious life, then tries to decipher its dynamism. Each of the "profiles" is presented through the contentions of a prominent, articulate advocate or spokesman, not all of whom are theologians or specialists in religious studies. In the first chapter, via the suggestions of Robert Jay Lifton, a psychiatrist, we shall examine some alternations between freedom and authority. In the second presentation, we shall deal with the contention of Norman O. Brown, a classicist well versed in the history of psychoanalysis, regarding the relationship of spirit and body. The third "profile" focuses directly upon the theology of hope and its depiction of the alternating currents of time and eternity, this world and a transcendent world. In each of eternity, this world and a transcendent world. In each a prominent previous religious emphasis has been reversed. Certainly the several profiles do not present the subject from the same standpoint or in the same light. Yet each of them provides a dramatic instance of alternation. Each is an example of what happens to religious enthusiasms when their theoretical or conceptual orientations are altered, or, in this case, dramatically transformed, and, indeed, inverted. The significant fact is that religious aspiration is not destroyed in the process, but only rediscovered and then redressed. The astounding fact is that faith appears to be rejuvenated even when made dependent upon a contrary vision of things. Following the profiles, we have engaged in some critical analysis, beginning with an examination of the religious mood James E. Dittes calls "positive disengagement." The analysis is calculated to support the view that though times are changing, change is neither so irregular nor so haphazard that there can be no grasp of its structure or penetration of its grammar.

The book is also an extended commentary on the career of the theology of hope, a theology which has played a major role in defining and articulating Christian religious aspiration in the current era. Simply from the point of view of theological reconstruction—the restructuring of conceptual categories, the interposition of time tenses, the conversion of vertical dimensionality into horizontal extention—the theology of hope has served as an unusually significant catalyst. And yet the theology of hope has also been influenced by the currents of alternation to which we have referred. It was an orientation born in 1965, reconstituted in 1974, but still active and vital, though in different terms and on another basis. The movement from political theology to a renewed interest in spirituality, symbolically, from Jürgen Moltmann, the political theologian, to Thomas Merton, the West's most influential fashioner of contemporary spirituality, does not make the original hope directives ineffectual or obsolete. On the contrary, just as Kantian philosophy argues that percepts without concepts are blind while concepts without percepts are empty, so too is there an inextricable and necessary interrelationship between a theology of action and a theology of contemplation. Without action, openness to contemplation is less knowing, and because of contemplation appreciation for action can be larger. That these two dominant currents are alternating but not mutually destructive is implicit in the title "hope against hope"—the same word appears on both sides of the contrast. The word "against" signifies that "hope" may not be subject to a single interpretation.

Some of the material included in the following chapters was originally designed for a set of alumni lectures given at Pacific Lutheran University in Tacoma. I am grateful to the faculty and students there for the honor that was bestowed on me, and to former President and Mrs. Eugene Wicgman, Harvey Neufeld, and Alfred and Esther Aus for their gracious hospitality. The same subjects have also been treated from time to time in lectures in the Franciscan Old Mission in Santa Barbara, conferences sponsored by the Wartburg Academy of the West in Thousand Oaks, and in an institute arranged by the Lutheran Institute for Theological Education in Portland. I am grateful to the many persons who have witnessed earlier readings of some of the chapters, from whose comments, suggestions, and encouragement I have benefited greatly. Particular thanks are due to Tina Keene and Deborah Sills for helping type the manuscript. My deepest thanks go to Jürgen Moltmann for providing visible proof that theology is conceivable in a new key.

Walter H. Capps
Santa Barbara, California

NOTES

1. I believe it possible to chronicle the recent development of programs in religious studies on state university campuses as an extension of Tillich's theological influence. Tillich's living presence in Santa Barbara at the strategically most appropriate time, for example, added immensely to the development and acceptance of the program. But the influence is even larger: throughout the country, those responsible for initiating academic programs in religious studies acknowledge large Tillichian leanings and dependencies.

2. Dietrich Bonhoeffer, *Letters and Papers from Prison,* ed. Eberhard Bethge, trans. Reginald H. Fuller (New York: Macmillan, 1953).

3. Harvey Cox, *The Secular City* (New York: Macmillan, 1965).

4. This theme, to which Novak returns again and again in his writings, is made the subject of several paragraphs in his *Ascent of the Mountain, Flight of the Dove* (New York: Harper and Row, 1971), pp. 24ff. The sense of his attitude is captured in the following sentences: "Holding a twig in one's hands, or a flower, one finds oneself absorbed in its singularity, its own inexhaustibility, its *haecceitus,* its own utter distinctness from oneself: it, not one's own ego, feelings, needs, is allowed to be the center of attention. Suddenly the world seems overridingly mysterious. Dimensions beyond dimensions are revealed in it. Nothing is too simple, too ordinary, too routine, to escape one's wonderment. Even the repetitions and rhythms of nature catch one's astonishment and attract one's imitation" (p. 41).

5. Jürgen Moltmann, *Theologie der Hoffnung* (Munich: Chr. Kaiser Verlag, 1965), published in English as *Theology of Hope: On the Ground and Implications of a Christian Eschatology,* trans. James W. Leitch (New York: Harper and Row, 1967).

6. This refers to the meeting of 18 Christian thinkers, representing nine denominations or churches, at the Hartford Seminary Foundation in Connecticut, in early February 1975, which was motivated by an interest in condemning thirteen current ideas which have the effect of undermining "transcendence." As the report in *Time* (February 10, 1975), put it: "In 1,150 words, their statement takes issue with some of the most popular liberal fashions of the past decade, including secular Christianity, political eschatology and the human potential movement."

Among those theses listed as being "false and debilitating" are the following: "The sole purpose of worship is to promote individual self-realization and human community. The world must set the agenda for the Church; social, political and economic programs to improve the quality of life are ultimately normative for the Church's mission in the world. An emphasis on God's transcendence is at least a hindrance to, and perhaps incompatible with, Christian social concern and action. The struggle for a better humanity will bring about the Kingdom of God. The question of hope beyond death is irrelevant or at best marginal to the Christian understanding of human fulfillment." The intrigue created by the Hartford meeting derives from the fact that many of the signers of this "Appeal for Theological Affirmation" had recently held views which the Appeal finds erroneous. As the *Time* report puts it: "Though the Hartford discussions brought out many theological differences, conservatives and liberals alike agreed on the necessity of Christian social involvement. However, a paradox was noted. The declaration insists that politically based theologies, which were created to foster social impact, have done just the opposite. . . . The view from Hartford is that Christianity will be too weak for a sustained attack on social evils—or for anything else—unless it first seeks the transcendence, power and will of God." An updated report on responses to the Hartford conference is included in the September 29, 1975 issue of *Newsweek*, p. 64.

7. Walter H. Capps, *Time Invades the Cathedral* (Philadelphia: Fortress Press, 1972).

PART ONE

PROFILES

CHAPTER ONE

THE ADVENT OF
THE PROTEAN STYLE

For the children . . . they sense it: there is no one over them; believable authority has disappeared; it has been replaced by experience. . . . The parents of these children, the fathers still believe in "someone" over them, insist upon it . . . demand it for and from their children. The children themselves cannot believe it; the idea means nothing to them.

—Peter Marin[1]

Shifts in theological orientation have come swiftly in the modern era. There have been numerous movements, tendencies, fashions, and fads, and these have come along, almost pell-mell, one after the other, rapidly and unceasingly. Some of these developments have not exhibited great staying power, even though some have been uncommonly creative. As a consequence, anyone who has tried to keep up to date by keeping abreast of the entire sequence has placed himself in breathtaking quests: almost as soon as he catches hold of the current he discovers that the rules, boundaries, and game plan have been altered.

But theological transformations and ecclesiastical shifts, as important as they are, may be secondary to the transformations—the tuggings and pullings—that have happened to persons inwardly. One thinks of the effects of the conflicts within the churches, the uncertain personal conviction of many priests and pastors, the nagging questions about personal and vocational religious identity, the inner rumblings and grumblings, and the kind of religio-political polarities that threaten to tear Christian communities apart. Though it came early, the Glock-Ringer-Babbie analysis of the churches, *To Comfort and to Challenge*,[2] still ranks as one of the most intelligent sociological examinations of this situation. *To Comfort and to Challenge* documented the view that churches motivated toward dispensing and insuring personal religious comfort become "successful" churches while those which find their *raison d'être* in challenging the socio-political status quo often achieve those goals only at the expense of the loss of their traditional membership constituencies. As a result, religious enthusiasms are deflected. In the one case, when religious commitment is enunciated, it seems to be directed toward goals that appear to be self-serving. In the other case, commitment is evoked and directed toward goals that some find worthy, but not all devotees construe as being religious. As a result, religious sensitivities remain pointed toward commitment and devotion, but without knowing what it is we are or ought to be committed to.

How does one sort out the many ingredients in this vast array? As a start, would it be fair to refer to Maurice Blondel's analysis of the fundamental religious dilemma? Writing almost a century ago, in France, Blondel professed that the goal is to find "a religion of inner freedom and external authority."[3] By this declaration, Blondel acknowledged that he wanted to protect external structure or authority, but not at the expense of internal freedom, by which he meant, in part, freedom of conscience. Freedom and authority were to be held in delicate balance.

Then, would it be fair to comment that, as neat and noble as Blondel's request may be, it is just the inverse of the current intention? At the present time the goal may be to

4

discover, construct, or create a religion of internal authority and external freedom. The intent is the inverse of Blondel's because of the overpowering increase of external freedom—the freedom to tinker with ecclesiastical forms, forms of worship, liturgical forms, religious life styles, and sociopolitical dispositions. It may be argued further that current external freedom has expanded at such a rapid rate that what is lacking, by contrast, is inner authority, deep-seated personal conviction, what Kierkegaard referred to as "subjectivity is truth."

The reasons for this may lie in the force with which change has occurred in the past several years. Or it may well be that change itself has been trying desperately to cope with the restructuring of human consciousness, urging such restructuring to occur sequentially rather than instantaneously and, thus, cataclysmically. At any rate, regardless of the reasons for it, one can suggest that our task is to find a religion of external freedom coupled with inner authority in which neither is achieved at the expense of the other. Some say we've achieved the former; but lack the latter. Perhaps it is that in the achievement of the first we've lost hold of the second, and that it does us little good to have either without the other.

One can test this possibility through the assistance provided by the psychiatrist, Robert Jay Lifton, and the work he has done in personality theory.[4] In his recent works, Lifton has announced that our age has witnessed the birth of a new kind of person, protean man, whose orientation to reality is calculated to cope with pervasive change. Indeed, protean man has been formed by change, perhaps even conceived by change. Thus, in analyzing the deportment of protean man we can perceive something of how the attempt to cope with change also affects the personality.

The designation "protean man" derives from the figure of Proteus, in Greek mythology, who, as tradition has it, was the prophetic old man of the sea and shepherd of the sea's flocks. According to Homer, Proteus lived off the island of Pharos, near the mouth of the Nile River. Virgil placed him near the island of Carpathus, between Rhodes and Crete. According to tradition, Proteus knew all things past, present, and future, but was reluctant to tell what he knew. Those who wanted to share in his wisdom had first to find him and then trap him. And this they could do around noontime when Proteus would take a nap in a cave by the sea surrounded by his seals. But when caught, Proteus would seek to escape by assuming all sorts of shapes. On occasion he could become a lion, a serpent, a leopard, a boar, a tree, sometimes even fire and water. And he could shift from one to the other and back again. Nevertheless, when seized by his captor, if held fast, Proteus would assume his proper shape, give the requested answer, then plunge into the sea. According to tradition, because of his ability to assume whatever shape he pleased, Proteus came to be regarded as a symbol of the original matter from which the world was created.

Lifton became disposed toward "Proteus" after conducting a series of interviews in 1962 with survivors of the atom bomb explosion at Hiroshima.[5] His general thesis is that the Hiroshima experience shatters the traditional boundaries by means of which men get some sense of the meaning of life and death. Because the extent of destruction is almost immeasurable, "those who experienced the bomb described it as a permanent encounter with death."[6] All of Hiroshima was involved in it; no person was exempt; and those who survived the phenomenon continued living "as though they were dead." Hiroshima had no precedent. There were no

6

prescriptions about how persons should behave under atom bomb attacks, nor about how persons should deal with it psychologically and emotionally. "The problem is magnified," Lifton says, "by the realization that any future war will be like Hiroshima, though on an even grander scale."[7] In short, by their very nature, men struggle to establish and maintain a definite boundary between the living and the dead. This boundary is implicit in our notions of immortality and in our aspirations toward salvation. But the boundary is shattered by the holocaust that affects an entire people or an entire civilization. And because of it one can no longer achieve a sense of rightness about things. There is no longer a way to establish adequate measures or proper balances. Lifton observes that there are no social balances, no natural balances, and no balance of things in nature.

The result is the advent of protean man. In fact, Lifton extrapolates on the personality traits of those conditioned by holocausts and Hiroshima—regarded fundamentally as the same sort of events—to describe the new man of our age. Unlike earlier men, protean man changes his ideological proclivities frequently. Earlier man may have undergone conversion, for example, but if he did he would have done it once, and it would have been a radical turnabout for him. It wouldn't have been something he would do over and over again. Once would have been for all time. But protean man acts differently. He undergoes conversion not just once and not just radically but frequently, repeatedly, and relatively. For protean man, world views, religious stances, and philosophical ideo-schemes are there to be embraced, modified, let go, withheld, reembraced, and all of this without necessary inner struggle. In fact, protean man can give allegiance to a point of view he once held, then left behind, knowing full well that he will probably abandon the position as soon as another attractive one comes into view, and will continue this tendency indefinitely. Lifton describes protean man as being "incapable of maintaining allegiance to just one ideology."[8]

But this is simply another way of documenting the contention that protean man has reference to a self-concept in motion. According to Lifton the protean style is a "self-process endless in its experiments and explorations."[9] And, for that reason, it is a self affected with "identity confusion" (in Erik Erikson's language).[10] Thus, with reference to what he has said about the significance of boundaries, Lifton can depict protean man as the representation of a "new style of self-process in our day," a style which implies "changing self-definitions" as well as a "blurring of perceptions of where self begins and ends." The connection with the disruption of boundaries becomes explicit.

The stimuli are several. Lifton makes much of contemporary man's having been afflicted with "historical and/or psychohistorical dislocation," by which he has reference to "the break in the sense of connection men have with the vital and nourishing symbols of their cultural traditions (symbols about family, idea systems, religions, and the human life cycle in general)." Protean man is not able to retain a sense of place. This is due to the freedom and ease with which men move about and shift locations. Ernst Bloch would have it that we have difficulty placing, reaching, or coming home. But the problem of "historical and psychohistorical dislocation" is compounded by the "flooding of imagery" which accrues through the development of mass media. During the course of a single television newscast, for example, a viewer can locate himself in any one of several geographical, cultural, and political environments. And there is no necessity that he identify solely or everlastingly with any one of them nor that he follow the sequence of movement that regulates the list of places "visited" during the newscast.

Lifton also lists some telling factors regarding protean man's attitude. For example, he notes that protean man is committed to the idea of making everything new, and this requires the transformation of everything. But, at the same time, protean man exhibits a general nostalgia to return to the "mythical past of perfect harmony and prescientific wholeness."[11] In other words, he wants to have it both ways. He is regulated by what Bloch calls the *novum,* by the fascination with new things, and particularly with new forms. But he is also intrigued by restorationism; that is, he senses that something valuable from the past has been lost and he seeks, primarily by means of exercises in "experiential transcendence," to recover the loss by merging it simultaneously with the new. Thus, through techniques of expanded consciousness, protean man attempts to co-mingle the immortal and the innovative. In so doing, he gives expression to the attitude that anything of any past human value can be recovered by experience in the here-and-now regardless of what it was or where we are. Thus, protean man's interest in the Buddha, for example, is not the simple historical fascination with the origin of a world-significant religious tradition; on the contrary, protean man's interest in the Buddha would be regulated by the prospect that Buddha's experience of enlightenment is repetitive and could be experienced and probed by those who are seeking to eliminate the boundaries of the self today. The same conviction would express itself in attitudes toward Jesus, the medieval mystics, and the other well-known commentators on consciousness-expanding Christian religious experience. In every such instance protean man will not be content simply to recapture the sense of a historical situation. Nor would he be satisfied in taking on historical case studies, or in learning how to place events in proper historical contexts. Rather, meaningful senses of history are made evident only when one discovers those senses in personal reexperience.

There are other notable features about protean man which we should try to understand. Lifton talks about the "breakdown of the boundaries of mentorship and authority" in which syndrome protean man participates. He makes it clear that he is thinking about relationships between fathers and sons. Given protean man's outlook, it is difficult to distinguish the relative ages of sons and fathers, for example, or, for that matter, daughters and mothers, because of the worlds available to expanded consciousness. The sons teach the fathers about realities the fathers have not yet experienced and may never experience. And, according to the sons' point of view, the fathers' teachings about other realities hold no conviction unless the fathers can also exhibit as much psychic awareness as the sons have. Once again, experience is the norm, and the premium is placed upon expanded consciousness. Mentorship is self-validating when it gives expression to "experiential transcendence." The same situation applies within the classroom. Teachers are experiential elders, not necessarily chronologically prior. "Students" teach "teachers" about things teachers have not experienced, and "teachers" can only appeal to ranges of shared experiences.

Furthermore, while protean man has come into being, as it were, because of a loss of connection with our primary symbolic environments, protean man is not content to leave ritual and liturgy behind. Lifton observes that protean man insists upon "rites of passage" to accompany his entry into birth, adulthood, marriage, and death. But, at the same time, protean man regards traditional rites and liturgies as being artificial, shallow, and fragmentary. Thus, wanting them but not accepting them, protean man makes up his own rituals. Lifton cites hippie weddings and Hindu incantations as cases in point. It is also significant, however one looks at it, that this is at least a tacit argument on behalf of the natural necessity of rituals and ritual systems. Even protean man, whose self-process consists of "a functional pattern necessary to life today,"[12] confesses that he cannot get along without symbolic structures, rituals, liturgies, and myths.

Much more can be said about protean man. It suffices here simply to sketch the gist of Lifton's argument, and then to convey some aspects of it that bear particularly on the matter of contrariness. We should recall the sequence. We begin with a swift reference to some of the more important developments within Christian theological and ecclesiastical circles during the past decade. We next came to focus on a widespread personal religious challenge or dilemma, that is, the difficulty many have correlating external freedom with inner authority (to reverse the Blondelian couplings). Thus, in turning to Lifton's account of protean man, we came to consider a model of personality formation which is prominent in our time for whom similar or analogous sets of inner dispositional proclivities seem both formative and characteristic. Now we must review Lifton's criticisms of protean man, and then we shall relate his and our analyses, if we can, to the principal theme of this book.

Lifton has ambivalent feelings about protean man. He gives cautious approval to protean man's objectives, or perhaps it is more accurate to refer to his view as a combination of applause and worry. On the one hand, Lifton appreciates how it was that protean man came to be. But,

11

on the other hand, he is not confident that protean man can find self-fulfillment via the style of life he is attempting to cultivate. Lifton cites several factors, all of which point to vulnerabilities in protean man's reflective, aesthetic, and emotional orientations. For example, Lifton finds it highly questionable that the forms of human culture can be recreated—or created anew—out of present psychic states. In pointing at this, Lifton is criticizing the view that experience is either self-validating, or, in more comprehensive terms, life-validating, and that consciousness has formative capacities which can be directed toward every endeavor, regardless of substance. The same weakness is implicit in the general tendency to replace history with experience. Lifton chalks this up to the romanticism of youth; he praises both youth and romanticism, and yet he finds this attitude to be naive. In this way he approaches protean man's aversion toward technology, materialism, bureaucracy, structure, system, establishment, and the like. Lifton holds some sympathy with romantic, youthful protean man on this point —almost as though he wished it were so—and yet he knows it deceptive to think that happily disposed inner feelings can take care of technological problems. There are large pitfalls implicit in the "temptation to transcend the system by romantic worship of the will as such." As carefully conceived strategy, this simply will not do.

To understand his deeper attitude toward protean man, one must be aware of the psychological claims that Lifton attempts to register. His first intention was to identify a prominent, contemporary model of personality formation. This he understands protean man to be. In addition, he wanted reliable assistance in understanding and appreciating the values and attitudes of young people today. Here again he argues that young people are fundamentally protean. So, he believes he has found success on both fronts. He has identified a dominant contemporary model of personality formation which provides him with an ability to characterize young people. Whereas previous models of personality formation were based on identifications of permanence, the protean model is designed to articulate with change.

Beyond the summary evaluations already mentioned, all of which refer in one way or another to the difficulties inherent in seeking to derive form, style, and code, without mediation, from psyche, Lifton offers some rather astute psychological observations which tend to put the subject into meaningful perspective. Almost in passing, he mentions that protean man is one "for whom there is no superego." In this regard he quotes Jean-Paul Sartre:

I left behind me a young man who did not have time to be my father, and who could now be my son. Was it a good thing or bad? I don't know. But I readily subscribe to the verdict of an eminent psychoanalyst, I have no Superego.[13]

In another place, Lifton offers a comment on the disappearance of superego in protean man: "Protean man requires a symbolic form of fatherlessness in order to carry out his explorations."[14] Thus, protean man is not regulated by absolute moral or ethical standards. He retains no ability to invoke comprehensive explanations or an overarching pattern of meaning. As a result, he seeks substitutes for all of this in various forms of psychological gratification.

It is clear that some alteration in the roles formerly assigned to what Freud referred to as ego, superego, and id is implicit in the transition that Lifton chronicles. We recall that in Freudian theory these three dimensions or structures of the psyche, these layers of consciousness, have different functions and play various roles, all three of which are necessary to psychological health or wholeness. In Freudian analysis id has reference to the reservoir of instinctive drives (or unconscious motivating power, or "libidinal energy"); ego provides the individual with specific direction, forges the individual's developmental history, and serves as the controlling agent, the *rational* element, which masters, synthesizes, and correlates experience; and superego is defined as "the moral factor which predominates the ego" by which Freud made reference to the "internal representation of the principles that regulate the child's and the adult's relation to the human environment."[15] While strict identification or equation is not intended, it is not incorrect to associate id with emotional sexual energy, ego with rationality, and superego with conscience. And in addressing this subject, one must always be aware that the Freudian trichotomy belongs to a theory, a theory that was composed to accompany an attempt to find the roots of pathological (neurotic or psychotic) behavior. Freud argued tirelessly that the superego is not itself conscience, for the function of superego is to a high degree unconscious. Nevertheless, given all of these appropriate qualifications, it remains true that, according to Freud, one's conscious life (one's mental and psychological well-being) involves a continuous interplay among the original instinctive drives (the id), the rational, refereeing element (the ego), and the inner representation of the structure and character of external reality (the superego).

Before exploring Lifton's contention that protean man is one for whom there is no superego, we must also consider the prospect, as has been suggested frequently, that religious persons—religiously sensitive people—characteristically exhibit exceptionally strong or influential superegos. These are persons who find it difficult, if not impossible, to go contrary to conscience, or to violate the structures of authority repeatedly and persistently. To turn the matter the other way, religious persons are frequently those for whom there is a strong abiding authority structure. They own a vital, deep-seated connection with an underlying symbolic environment in which relationships of fathers to sons, mothers to daughters, parents to children, and children to parents are prescribed. To put the matter more simply, in Freudian terms, this tends to reflect the psychological situation which serves as preparation or occasion for belief in God. Some observant people have also discovered that strong adherence to superego sometimes implies underdevelopment of other aspects of the personality. David Bakan argues, for example, that St. Augustine's views on sex were negotiated finally through the sacrifice of the id to the ego and superego.[16] It is clear also that some adolescent religious dilemmas—clashes between faith, reason, doubt, for example—reflect internal personal tension. In such struggles one aspect of the self is in conflict with another, superego with ego, superego with id, etc. I refer specifically to those compulsions toward personal religious commitment which demand that rationality be subsumed under (or sacrificed to) conscience, or even to the repression of personal feelings because of the overpowering presence of conscience. As Bakan recognizes, it is certainly true that libidinal energy has gone unrecognized, undernourished, even thwarted or dissipated because of strong religious orientations to superego. Many who have been so affected have attempted to compensate for that initial orientation by tapping the unconscious, laying bare the things that lie unperturbed in those drives that are sometimes made apparent only in our jokes, art, dream life, or, to paraphrase Alfred North Whitehead, in "what one does with his solitariness." Many such persons have honored the belief that previous forms of personal religiousness have demanded a rigorous tending to the things of the superego at all costs, even if that implies sacrifice of the id.

Protean man reverses all of this. He is the one for whom there is no superego, one who celebrates the birth and/or discovery of the id, and one whose life strategy is based on the capacities of the id to create meaningful form through the recognition and extension of its playful, energetic, and potentially romantic largesse.

As one listens to Lifton he cannot help but suspect that protean man is necessary to nullify previous imbalances. It is possible, isn't it, to so identify being religious with being dutiful, or with holding correct religious beliefs, that persons obey authority without ever discovering who they are? The same would be impossible for protean man. And if protean man fosters this awareness, whatever else he does, he can also prompt us toward greater religious maturity.

And yet the new protean insights must follow contrariness's rule. For the necessary alternations are present both in protean man's reaction against a previous authoritarianism and in Lifton's guarded criticism of protean man. To turn from permanence to change, from authority to freedom, from superego to id, provides untold advantages, and it also leaves one looking for a new sort of permanence and a refined, updated, dynamic, and more resilient basis of authority. When religious orientations are significantly altered, gains are made at the expense of conditions necessarily shunted aside.

NOTES

1. Peter Marin, "The Open Truth and Fiery Vehemence of Youth," *Center Magazine* 2, No. 1 (1969): 72.

2. Charles Y. Glock, Benjamin B. Ringer, and Earl R. Babbie, *To Comfort and To Challenge* (Berkeley: University of California Press, 1967).

3. Maurice Blondel, *L'Action: Essai d'une Critique de la Vie et d'une Science de la Pratique* (Paris: Bibliothèque de Philosophie Contemporaine, Felix Alcan, 1893). See the bibliography on Blondell included in J. J. McNeill, *The Blondelian Synthesis* (Leiden: E. J. Brill, 1966).

4. Robert Jay Lifton, *Boundaries. Psychological Man in Revolution* (New York: Random House, 1970).

5. Lifton, *Death in Life. Survivors of Hiroshima* (New York: Random House, 1968).

6. Lifton, *Boundaries*, p. 4.

7. Ibid., p. 17.

8. Ibid., p. 53.

9. Ibid., p. 44.

10. Ibid., p. 43.

11. Ibid., p. 60.

12. Ibid., p. 44.

13. Ibid., p. 47.

14. Ibid., p. 48.

15. Sigmund Freud's most concise treatment of the interrelationship of superego, ego, and id is to be found in Chapter III ("The Ego and the Superego") of *The Ego and the Id*, trans. Joan Riviere, ed. James Strachey (New York: W. W. Norton, 1960), pp. 18–29. One of his most lucid renderings of the same interrelationship is presented in *Civilization and its Discontents*, trans. James Strachey (New York: W. W. Norton, 1961), especially pp. 72ff.

16. David Bakan, "Some Thoughts on Reading Augustine's *Confessions*," *Journal for the Scientific Study of Religion* 5, No. 1 (1965): 149–152.

CHAPTER TWO

THE RECOVERY
OF THE BODY

Unless one becomes as a little child, he cannot enter the
kingdom of heaven.

—Jesus of Nazareth[1]

In the previous chapter, we focussed on a significant,
recent shift in the conception of the relationship of life and
death, and we noticed that the same shift is present in the
conception of the meaning of freedom and authority. We
considered the intrinsic dynamism of that relationship, noting its influence upon the creation of a new model of personality formation, a figure Robert Lifton has called "protean man." We proceeded to suggest that, in many respects,
our age can be called a protean age because of the prevalence of this personality type in life all around us. We
observed that religious orientation could and has been reconstituted in protean terms. And we concluded that the
reversal or transposition of priorities was in no way destructive, but merely shifted religious enthusiasms to another
base. Religion prospers in the protean age through sensitivity to the dictates of the id rather than the superego.

In this chapter we shall pursue the same theme, that is,
the transposition of emphasis within a specific set of contraries, though with a different focus. Our spokesman this
time is Norman O. Brown, whose analyses, like Lifton's,
reflect a Freudian orientation. In moving from Lifton to
Brown, we are shifting our attention from the relationship

of life and death to the relation of spirit and body. Yet, though the focus is different, we are dealing with another example of binary alternation. Whereas earlier religious formulation found spirit to be the term of major stress, and body as a matter for subordination, Brown champions body, maintaining the same relational set. What follows is a summary of his story.[2]

All of us, it seems, are aware of conflict. Sometimes the conflicts are small. Sometimes they are larger. Sometimes they appear trifling. Sometimes they take on larger magnitudes. We learn about conflicts when we are forced to choose between two or more incompatible versions of a story. We engage conflict when we encounter opposition to our own well-laid plans. Conflict implies disharmony, incompatibility, opposition, antagonism, and hostility. It occurs in a variety of forms and within a variety of contexts. There are personal conflicts, interpersonal conflicts, intrapersonal conflicts, corporate conflicts, international conflicts, world conflicts, ecological conflict, environmental conflict, even cosmic and cosmological conflict. Indeed, many religious analyses of the human predicament begin by focussing on conflict. What is significant about the human situation, in these accounts, is that man is immersed in conflict. He must respond to a conflicted world. Confliction is thus the basic fact about man's being in the world, and it signifies deception, distortion, and the need to become reoriented.

Because conflict is such a pervasive fact, all of us feel some obligation to account for it. Or, as some interpretation has it, conflict may be attributed to the natural opposition between the forces of good and the forces of evil, that is, to clashes between the children of light and the children of darkness. Sometimes there is conflict because different ages view things differently, because there are gaps between generations. Sometimes it is a matter of difference in attitude and outlook between adolescents and adults, or between persons with differing cultural horizons. All sorts of theories of explanation can be suggested. The interpretations can be multiplied. And yet, none of them eliminate conflict. Conflict is prominent and appears inevitable in the world in which we live.

Many analysts, both professional and otherwise, ancient and modern, have proposed that our conflict is due to the fact that the body is at odds with the spirit. It is easy to explain this by suggesting that the body is a *drag* on the soul—something which weighs or pulls it down, a heavy burden which keeps the soul in subjection and prevents it from soaring high or flying away into uncharted lands of thought and consciousness. From here, it is easy to estimate the body as being of lesser value than the soul. Or, to turn the matter the other way, the spirit is regarded as being more real and of having greater lasting importance than the body. In contrast to the spirit, the body, despite all appearances to the contrary, really becomes something less than real. One remembers the biblical statement: "all flesh is grass, and the grass withers, the flower fades. . . ." The explanations and interpretations of conflict often lead this way: the body and the spirit are juxtaposed. Hence, conflict cannot be thoroughly externalized, for it really implies that man is at odds with himself.

Brown knows of this analysis, and he invests in it heavily. But for him the outcome is just the reverse. In the binary relationship of body and spirit, the emphasis is shifted to the reality of the body. And the suggestion is that conflict is resolved through the enunciation—not renunciation—of bodily desires.

Brown's account of human conflict takes the following

form. He is mindful first that other interpretations of human conflict are quick to begin by creating a subject-object dichotomy. In these formulations the conflict is explained on the basis of the opposition between the subject and some contrary external reality. Opposed to treating conflict as subject-object tension, Brown counters with the contention that the real conflict occurs *within the subject*. He refers conflict to "dualisms of instincts inside the subject." That is, the prime conflict is to be rooted within the person. It does not occur between the self and some opposing element outside the self, but within the self, between two dimensions, aspects, or layers of one and the same person.

Certainly there are complex Freudian and post-Freudian contentions implicit here, as well as a long tradition of psychoanalysis, reflection, and commentary. Were we attempting a genetic account of Brown's theories, we would have to begin with Freud, and then spend considerable time with the infrequently cited contentions of Geza Roheim, whom the textbooks describe as one of the first anthropologists seriously to take up the theories of Freud.[3] Any strict historical account would show, as Brown acknowledges, that much of what he says about neurosis and culture was stimulated by Roheim's contention that "culture arises from man's neotenic retardation and biologically-delayed maturity." "Neotenic retardation" refers to the difference between *man* and animals by virtue of the fact that, in man's case, there is a significant gap between the time he attains sexual potency and the time he produces offspring. By contrast, as soon as they are sexually capable, animals simply reproduce. But the human species waits. And the waiting period is socially and culturally—not biologically—enforced.

But the strict historical account is not our task here.

21

Rather our purpose is to illustrate what happens within a primary binary relationship—this time, the relationship between body and spirit—when the expected relational stress is shifted to the other side. In this instance, Brown upholds the significance of "body" in the body-spirit binary relation instead of placing the stress where one has been trained to expect it, namely, on the word "spirit." And for this purpose it suffices that we more carefully explore the basic conflict which Brown seeks to unravel, and that we trace the alterations which follow.

To come to terms with this, one must try to picture the situation of the human baby. In infancy, a child is allowed to enjoy a variety of exercises and escapades in obvious "erotic pleasure." The little baby enjoys putting things in his or her mouth. He plays with himself. He tickles himself. He seems to enjoy being fondled. He enjoys sucking. When his stomach is full, he can enjoy his body. He delights in his body; he takes pleasure in his mother's body.

But, when one compares adult behavior with the behavior of infants, drastic changes are recognized. Before the child is very many months old, he learns with some real pain that thumb sucking is unacceptable behavior. Furthermore, one cannot engage in bodily poking, tickling, frisking, and the like, simply whenever one feels inclined to poke, tickle, and frisk. A child cannot engage in the full panoply of bodily delights whenever the child wants to. One is not allowed to suck anything or everything simply because sucking is pleasurable. No, one discovers that this isn't the way things are negotiated in polite society. One learns that thumb sucking is unacceptable behavior after one has reached a certain stage of bodily development. And so it goes: the early pleasures are taken away, one after another, all under the auspices of a drive toward normalcy or maturity. Maturity implies conformity to accepted or acceptable reality.

Now against this background, one can appreciate Brown's attraction to Roheim's suggestions. For what if it is true, as Roheim claims, following Freud, that cultures are suspiciously created in order to keep infantile urges repressed? Could it not be, as Roheim attests, that culture is a defense mechanism, by which mechanism neuroses are created and sustained? What if it is true, as Roheim states, that real maturity—not reality-principle defined maturity—really consists of regaining the "paradise lost" of infancy? In short, the child within each of us is being frustrated by a fabricated, substitutionary adult.

Our lives are narrow, shallow, and constricted because they have been formed by imposed artificial substitutionary norms. This is how Brown sees it. Our desire for happiness is frustrated because it is in conflict with reality. In more exact Freudian language, the compulsions of the "pleasure principle" are in opposition to the dictates of the "reality principle." To resolve the dilemma we repress the very essence of our being. We masquerade our true selves. We engage in charade-like adventures without acknowledging that they are charades. We allow ourselves to be motivated by compulsions that run contrary to our basic natures. We are in conflict with ourselves. We are detached and distended. Or as Brown says it, "only in the unconscious does the pleasure-principle reign supreme."[4]

Who then is man?—*homo sapiens*? *homo religiosus*? *homo symbolicus*? No, for Brown, "man is the animal which represses himself."[5] Following Roheim, "man is the animal whose biological maturity is retarded."[6] Even society is created to assist man in his efforts to repress himself, to restrict his true nature. But, contrary to reality-principle teachings, true satisfaction is not to be found in society.

Natural human drives and desires are not satisfied by society. To place such expectations upon the "reality principle" is to deceive oneself, and to accept a figment or an illusion for true reality. "In the secret places of his being," Brown writes, "man knows that he is motivated most of all not by reason but by delight."[7] And the sign of the illusory quality of the false reality is the effort we expend to prevent primary unconscious drives from rising to the level of consciousness. We repress the unconscious. We resist it. We disown it. We disavow it. And yet in following this pattern, we also resist, disown, disavow, and repress our truer and better selves.

This, briefly, is Brown's diagnosis. And he offers a solution, a response to the age-old question: "What doth it profit a man if he gains the whole world and loses the self?" Or as some versions have it, his *true* self. Or as Nicodemus asked in the Gospel account: "But how can one be born anew? Can one be born when he is old?"

Brown doesn't claim that his insights can be transposed into a scheme of salvation, but he does have some insights, and they sound very biblical. "One must be born anew," he says. "One must become as a little child,"—yes, a little child. One must return to infancy. For, as Brown sees it, our desires for happiness, which we have *repressed*, are the very desires we had, *unrepressed*, in childhood. And he adds, they are sexual desires. They pertained to the enjoyment of the body, and not just restricted body, partial body, qualified sexual body, but the whole, total body. Such delights point to comprehensive erotic delights, that is, the delights which were relinquished in favor of the injunctions of the reality principle.

Implications fall here, there, and everywhere. There are religious overtones alongside ramifications of other sorts.

For example, Brown says that the pattern of normal adult sexuality is not a natural (biological) necessity but a cultural phenomenon. And this is simply another way of saying that the usual patterns of accepted sexuality are concessions to the reality principle, which principle functions in turn to keep the primary desires repressed. Brown observes that *"the eternal child in us is frustrated by the tyranny of genital organization."*[8] Religion—institutional, social, reality-sanctioned religion—has been one of the chief, and most powerful forces of repression.

Brown's book, *Life Against Death*, has very many things to say about the tragedies that have come to Western and Eastern cultures because of religious influences. For instance, Brown argues that two thousand years of Western and religious history has trained man for *asceticism*. And, as Brown knows very well, ascetic practices tend to flourish when the world is viewed dualistically, when men understand their experience in the world to be regulated by dualistic opposition of soul and body. Persons engage in ascetic practices in order to purify their souls. The purification of souls or spirits is another way of talking about keeping spirits or souls unstained, unspotted, or besmirched—a wonderful word, *besmirched*—by the body. Most spiritual ascetic practices—silence, guarded thoughts, spiritual reading, prayer, obedience, the acceptance of humility—are designed to enhance the spiritual life and to keep it from falling victim to bodily delights and physical appetites. In fact, the ascetic practice of mortifying or crucifying the body—*mortificatio carnis*—is the physical form of purification of soul. One crucifies the body so that the soul does not come under its power or control. The assumptions are obvious.

Asceticism implies that man consists of a soul trapped in

a body. Asceticism also implies that the life of reason—man's spiritual or rational potentialities—is to be prized over everything physical. When these assumptions are extended, they add up to the contention that "the essence of man consists in disembodied mental activity." Man is most himself—he comes closest to what he is meant to be—when the soul is separated from the body. Then he is no longer affected by physical corruption. Much otherworldly asceticism has been regulated this way. This also has been the dominant teachings of many prominent religions. And it doesn't take much imagination to understand what all of it implies regarding matters sexual. Sexuality too is to be avoided, or at least held under suspicion, or at best *kept in its proper place*, because of its many threats to the pure life of the soul. Sexuality is tantamount to investments in corruption. It is base, because the physical is base, and we succumb to it only when we are able to keep ourselves from falling victim to bodily appetites. Religion, too, becomes asexual. The life of celibacy is to be prized above the life of sexual involvement. In fact, if the truth were known, religious interests carry all sorts of disguised sexual overtones. Religious enthusiasms are formed frequently out of diverted, redirected sexual drives. Religious talk is frequently disguised sexual talk. And the alternative Brown offers is not body-repressive spiritualism—anti-body religion—but a body-mysticism which affirms the primal awareness of the eternal child.

Parenthetically, I must say that I didn't know how seriously to take Brown in this regard until I had occasion, one time a few years ago, to travel to a church meeting in New York. On the flight across country I had been reading *Love's Body*, for my appetite had been whetted by one of Robert Bellah's reviews of the book.[9] So I came to the meeting of church officials and theologians with Brown's contentions very much on my mind. Much to my surprise, although Brown should have taught me to expect it, I found myself party to a lot of very high-level, sophisticated, and sanctioned talk about *bodies,* even about *bodily union.* To be sure, the bodies being referred to weren't human bodies; rather they were church bodies, ecclesiastical bodies. And, for almost two days the preponderance of talk was about merging this body with another body, about the possibility of union between one body and another body, and about the impractibility just now of a three-way bodily union. Apparently each one of the bodies in question enjoyed a capacity for union with either one of the other two bodies, but there seemed to be little prospect that the three bodies could "join in real organic union" with each other. Apparently in matters ecclesiastical, two is good company and three is a crowd. It is a straining of the organic categories to attempt a three-way union.

Brown could call all of this disguised or, perhaps overt sexual talk. And he might suggest that whereas religious persons find it difficult to engage in direct overt sexual talk, because it violates the premise that the spiritual is to be prized above the physical, they employ the same language more indirectly to talk about such sanctionable things as mergers, unions, and consummations of unions between ecclesiastical bodies. Perhaps this explains the preponderance of anal references in clerical jokes. Perhaps all of it flows from the fact that we repress our inmost selves. Yet, despite our best efforts, we cannot fully repress ourselves. To do it at all we must continue telling ourselves that the true essence of man consists in disembodied mental or spiritual activity.

Not so for Brown. On the contrary, for him the true

27

essence of man "lies in infantile sexuality." As we have
noted, he is fond of quoting Jesus' phrase, "Except one become as a little child he cannot enter the Kingdom of God."
Then he goes on to stay that many of the great religious personages understood this; he mentions Francis of Assissi, the
mystics, William Blake, the poet Rilke, and Rousseau—all
of these, he says, understood this truth.[10] They all recognize that being childlike expressed itself in a kind of ex-
uberant, spontaneous, rejoicing, self-gratifying celebration
of all of life. In other words, all of them knew that
"pleasure-principle" and "reality-principle" involve different
dispositions and employ different temperaments. And all
of them recognized that deep-seated religious needs are not
satisfied by the "economic activity and struggle for existence
(which are) dictated by the reality-principle." Instead, all
of them approached the world in a bouyant, playful attitude, recognizing with Johann Huizinga that play is the
attitude out of which the most meaningful things are created. Brown writes:

Play is the essential character of activity governed by the
pleasure-principle rather than the reality-principle. Play is "pur-
poseless yet in some sense meaningful." It is the same thing if
we say that play is the *erotic mode* of activity. Play is that
activity which, in the delight of life, unites man with the objects
of his love, as is indeed evident from the role of play in normal
adult genital activity . . . according to Freud, the ultimate
essence of our being is erotic and demands activity according
to the pleasure-principle.[11]

All along many folks thought it was the other way, that we
really come close to the heart of things when we are serious,
reflective, concerned, committed. A case in point is the
large following elicited by Paul Tillich's identification of
religion with "ultimate concern."

The difference can be spotted in a person's aspects. Reality-principle oriented persons are serious, reflective, and sometimes seem preoccupied with how they are being viewed, regarded, or evaluated by others. By contrast, those persons whom Brown commends have a certain ageless, timeless, youthful aspect. Priest friends of mine tell me that Brown's discussion of the relationship of being religious with childhood interests explains for them why so many of their fellows display an obvious boyish look. And when describing religious persons, Erik Erikson takes note of the fact that they frequently display unusual wisdom at a very early age and remain youthful even at advanced ages of life. Erikson writes in *Young Man Luther*:

He (*homo religiosus*) is always older, or in early years suddenly becomes older, than his playmates or even his parents and teachers, and focuses in a precocious way on what it takes others a lifetime to gain a mere inkling of. . . . Because he experiences a breakthrough to the last problems so early in his life maybe such a man had better become a martyr and seal his message with an early death. . . . We know little of Jesus of Nazareth as a young man, but we certainly cannot even begin to imagine him as middle-aged.[12]

All of this might be employed as testimony that the ultimate essence of our being is *erotic* and demands activity according to the pleasure-principle.

We can add example to example to indicate what might be meant by a shift from spirit to body emphasis within this fundamental binary relationship to which large portions of religious sensitivity are oriented. But then we would simply be adding example to example. Perhaps it is enough for us to note that an orientational shift has been recommended, and then to trace a few of the more prominent implications of that shift. After all, our task is not to build a case for Brown's contention, but rather to get the sense of what he is asserting. It suffices in this respect that we understand how he goes about his work, and how his interpretation articulates with one of the profound religious revolutions which has occurred around us during the past several years.

Having done all of that, we have done enough. But if I am allowed to add but one footnote, let me suggest the following with regard to Brown's seizing upon the word "body." I add this because the first time I met and heard Brown, a truly unforgettable experience, he made reference to the crucial significance of the last words of the New Testament. You remember those words, "Come quickly, Lord Jesus." He is serious about them. He believes in the apocalyptic age. He believes in an era of liberation. And he can read Jesus' interpretation of the Kingdom of God in precisely these terms. If you say to him, when will it come? how? where? in what form? he sometimes answers *Now*. But Now, in this instance, belongs to a timeless state (because it is located within the world of the id). And then he'll assert that he hopes that his and our children will see the fuller life. He professes that mankind has already entered a new phase. The path to human salvation via *sublimation* and *repression* has already run its course. There is no place else for it to go, except to stop, atrophy, to be replaced by another current, truer, more vital, resourceful, more distinctively human, more realistic, and supremely more promising path. He states that the only path available to mankind is "the path wherein the bonds between all the peoples of the world are based not on *aggression* and *anxiety*, but on *narcissism* and *erotic exuberance*." This is why all talk about human fulfillment and the end of the age comes to focus on *the resurrection of the body*. The salvation to which Christians bear testimony is not the sort that can be effected by separating purified souls from contaminated bodies, but *a salvation which occurs in the body*. Don't ask for details, for Brown expresses himself in aphorisms and in reworkings of the canons of the Latin Mass. In the new age, it is not appropriate to speak discursively. Within the context of the apocalyptic mode, it is impossible to prophesy in programmatic terms. Proposals cannot be laid out in step-by-step progression. But one thing is sure. Eternal life can only be life in a body, and this reality is dawning as a cultural fact. Brown writes:

The resurrection of the body is a social project facing mankind as a whole, and it will become a practical political problem when the statesmen of the world are called upon to deliver happiness instead of power, when political economy becomes a science . . . of enjoyment instead of a science of accumulation.[13]

In the next chapter we shall turn to another large alternation, this time between vertical and horizontal projection in the conception of the Christian life. This alternation affects the relationship between time and eternity, and it tends to place greater stress on the things of this earth than to the components of heaven. Such large consequences are reason enough to examine the alternations implicit in the theology of hope. But a greater intrigue concerns the resistance this alternation has met. It seemed for awhile that the theology of hope was going to achieve a revolution within Christian consciousness. Perhaps this did occur in fact. But, along the way, the revolution tended to dawdle, and a retrogressive movement from horizontal to vertical projection gathered increasing force. For this reason, we shall approach the next profile in sequence under the title "What ever happened to hope?"

NOTES

1. Matthew 18:3.

2. Norman O. Brown, *Life Against Death* (Middletown: Wesleyan University Press, 1959); *Love's Body* (New York: Random House, 1966); *Closing Time* (New York: Random House, 1973). See also Brown's *Hermes the Thief* (Madison: University of Wisconsin Press, 1947).

3. Geza Roheim, *The Origin and Function of Culture* (New York: Nervous and Mental Disease Monographs, No. 69, 1943). Two other works of Roheim are of particular significance in disclosing and developing his attitude toward religion. The first, *The Panic of the Gods, and Other Essays,* ed. Werner Muensterberger (New York: Harper and Row, 1972), contains a perceptive introductory chapter by Muensterberger. The second, *Psychoanalysis and Anthropology: Culture, Personality, and the Unconscious* (New York: International Universities Press, 1950), features a chapter on "The Unity of Mankind" (Chapter Ten) in which Roheim contends that man's prolonged infancy is the key to the understanding of human nature: ". . . human beings have conserved traits in the anatomical structure which makes them comparable to juvenile or foetal anthropoids" (p. 401).

4. Brown, *Life Against Death,* p. 8.

5. Ibid., p. 9.

6. Roheim, "The Evolution of Culture," *International Journal of Psychoanalysis* 15 (1934): 387–418.

7. Brown, *Life Against Death,* p. 9.

8. Ibid., p. 29.

9. Robert N. Bellah, *Beyond Belief* (New York: Harper and Row, 1970), pp. 230–236.

10. Brown, *Life Against Death,* p. 32.

11. Ibid., pp. 32–33.

12. Erik H. Erikson, *Young Man Luther* (New York: W. W. Norton, 1958), p. 261.

13. Brown, *Life Against Death,* pp. 317–318.

CHAPTER THREE

WHAT EVER HAPPENED TO HOPE?

Let us give Apocalypse a rest. We do not need it to tell us that our ways must mend, or that our business suffers from daily outrages. Pick up an issue of TIME, DAEDALUS, or COLLEGE ENGLISH. Purchase the latest radical reader or anti-text. . . . Yet how many see . . . that we now strike . . . at an older idea of man? . . . A post-humanism is in the making. What will be its shape?

—Ihab Hassan[1]

There was a time, not long ago—some of us remember it well—when people were excited about hope. This was a time when the excitement about hope was matched by careful theoretical support for hope. At that time, not long ago, it was possible both to hope and to know that hoping was the thing to do. There were persons who hoped, and there was widespread advocacy of hope. Each nurtured the other. Lots of people talked about hope. A number of scholars, teachers, and journalists wrote about hope. Hope was in the air, so to speak. It was in books. It was in music (usually to guitar accompaniment). So to speak, hope was in sermons. People discussed hope. They talked about it. Hope even inserted itself into deliberations regarding man's future. Often the concern about "the year 2000" was influenced by hope. But all of this was some time ago. Not so long ago. Some of us remember it. And then something happened.

What happened? Perhaps we'll never know. But something did happen. It happened to the persons who hoped. It happened to persons who talked, sang, and wrote about hope. It happened in books, no longer about hope. It happened to sermons, to music, to the concern about the future, to "the year 2000." It happened! What happened? What ever happened to hope?

At one time, it almost seemed as if Ernst Bloch, Jürgen Moltmann, Johannes Metz, and the others had unlocked a secret. It was as though they had discovered a way to get into the future before the future happened. It was as though one could live in the future while the future was still-not-yet. Then, having located the future tense, these advocates of hope fashioned means of tracing its presence everywhere. Theology could be regulated by the future tense, they suggested. And a theology so regulated could find strong philosophical supports. One's attitude to the fate of the world could be formed by the content of hope inserted into the category of the future. Human destiny could be construed this way. The meaning of history could be conceived this way. Optimism could be sustained this way. Aspirations could be expressed this way. It was appropriate to hope, and to recognize that hopeful was the way to be. In the view of the designers of the mood, this was not a new philosophy and theology. Rather it was a rediscovery and revitalization of an old and fundamental human current. It tapped a deep, important, and primordial human nerve. In Bloch's view, the philosophy of hope actually had roots in classical Greek philosophy, particularly in the fragments of Heraclitus. This was to claim good breeding, for Heraclitus is one of the most respected of ancient philosophers. It also places novelty within a long, sustaining tradition, for Heraclitus reaches back to the beginning of western, philosophical thought. This implies that

Bloch's suggestions were fundamentally reconstructive. The transformations he called for belong to a context which possessed an intellectual geneology of considerable depth and durability.

Following the philosopher Bloch, the theologian Moltmann asserted that hope had deep theological roots too. Not only was the recovery of hope philosophically and politically defensible, Moltmann argued, but the theme was central to the New Testament as well. Leave hope out, and the New Testament is not New Testament. Omit hope and the Christian Gospel is not Gospel. In Moltmann's reading, the New Testament refers throughout to the coming Kingdom of God. This is its dominant theme. The gospel depends upon the realization of the Kingdom of God. Thus, appreciation for hope leads one to the center of Christian affirmation. After all, isn't Christian salvation based on the hope that Jesus will return again? And doesn't this imply that someday the Kingdom of God will be realized, perhaps even visibly? And doesn't this constellation of affirmation and aspiration compel the Christian to envision the future expectantly? Moltmann thought so, in the awareness that he was thinking, rethinking, and reaffirming fundamental New Testament motifs anew.

The next step was to link the theology of hope to the philosophy of hope. Through this linkage, Bloch came to be looked upon not only as an interesting philosopher in his own right, but as a writer who had provided intriguing new images and arresting new clues regarding the meaning and interpretation of the New Testament. In an earlier day, Reinhold Niebuhr had talked about the need to keep the Bible and the *New York Times* beside one another on the desk, so that one's readings in each would be interpreted by the other. Now one could read the New Testament and

Bloch's *Das Prinzip Hoffnung*[2] in the same context. The two were expressions of a common theme, and, in many respects, were of the same genre. As those so motivated progressed with their simultaneous reading of Bloch and the Christian New Testament, a veritable new world opened for them. Not only were they enabled to root their Christian aspirations in durable and solid conceptual and scriptural bases, but they also came to be convinced that their aspirations were of real substance. The same intrigue, excitement, and anticipation was assisted by the fact that Bloch was himself not a Christian, but instead—is "instead" the correct word any longer?—a Jew who is of Marxist political and atheist religious persuasions. Think of it. The person who made it possible for Christians to rediscover a central and crucial theme in their own holy book is Jewish, Marxist, and atheist. That Bloch was the prime catalyst gave the new mood a luster, fascination, and intrigue as well as an instant working mythology. And, as an early side benefit, some Christians and some Marxists learned that they could join together for dialogue and conversation. But the primary event was that the hope school had detected, tapped, and manifested a large need. It was sensitive to the current mood. It understood and sympathized, and responded in strong, clear, and positive tones. Besides, it provided Christians with terminology to be used to articulate this newer experience.

It was interesting, too, that the advocates of the hope movement—at least many of those who played leadership roles—had been "oppressed persons" of one sort or another approximately two decades before. Two of the theological spokesmen for the movement had spent months in prisoner of war camps during the Second World War, Metz in Maryland and Moltmann in Scotland. Bloch himself had been an oppressed and "displaced person" time and again, usually because one or another (or the combination) of the labels by which he was identified were not acceptable. The "oppressed person" motif is even stronger because of the influence of Dietrich Bonhoeffer, whom theologians of hope frequently cited as implicit precedent for their own contentions. Indeed, one could gather strong support for the interpretation that the theology of hope is Bonhoeffer's theology extended and developed. In 1964, twenty years after Bonhoeffer's death, it was still important to assert that "the world must come of age." Interestingly, the writings to which the geneological references frequently are made are to Bonhoeffer's prison writings, *The Letters and Papers from Prison*.[3] Significantly, Bloch's *Das Prinzip Hoffnung* and Bonhoeffer's *Letters and Papers* were written at about the same time. Many of their themes overlap in striking ways. Both bespeak "oppression," and both tie human salvation to release from bondage.

Thus the link to the biblical exodus tradition was not difficult to establish. *Das Prinzip Hoffnung* announced a present exodus by which was implied release from bondage, a new corporate liberation, and a willingness to refer one's identity to an unfolding promising future. Speaking autobiographically of the prisoner of war camp origins of the theology of hope, Moltmann recalls:

As I continue to look back I see a young prisoner of war interned in an English camp. His horizon there is the barbed wire, even though the war had been over for some time. His path is one which curves in a circle around the edges of the barbed wire. Freedom lies beyond—out there where people live and laugh. To be sure, this prisoner was not in a morgue, as was Dostoevski in Siberia. Externally, at any rate, the internment camp was bearable. But hope rubbed itself raw on the barbed wire! A man cannot live without hope! I saw men in the camp who lost hope. They simply lay down, took ill, and died. When life's hopes flounder and crack up, a sadness beyond comforting sets in. But on the other hand, hope disturbs and makes one restless. One can no longer be content with his situation, with the way things are. Every little thing becomes a prison. One lives only for repatriation. That's all one dreams of. One becomes moody, impatient, often cynical. One cannot live—often, not even survive—without hope. But even this hope becomes the prisoner's torment. The prisoner experienced an inner conversion when he gave up hope of getting home soon, and in his yearning he rediscovered that deeper "hope against hope." Hope made him free to accept, even laugh at the barbed wire, and to discover in his fellow prisoners human beings whose company he enjoyed, with whom he could be happy even in suffering. An American periodical once stated that the theology of hope was born in a prisoner of war camp. Autobiographically speaking, I believe it may have been correct. But the hope that was born there was not that painful, disturbing hope, but rather a deeper, liberating hope which works through love.

Moltmann continues on, recalling what it was like to return to his war shattered country, and then to enroll in theological studies:

Still looking back, I see myself as a young student of theology who had returned home in 1948 with the hope for a new, more humane Germany, and for a liberated, liberating church of Christ. . . . The survivors of my generation came into the lecture halls from hospitals and prisoner of war camps inwardly shattered, from flesh bearing all the marks of war. . . . During the post-war period we were, politically speaking, opposed to the restoration of things as they had been. So far as the church was concerned, we turned to renewal movements. I experienced the difficulty of this struggle between restoration and renewal out of the true origin while I was the pastor of a small congregation. At that time restoration meant a denial or suppression of the memory of Germany's terrible past, and of the many accommodations of the church to the rule of the Beast. Renewal meant for us the acknowledgement of our guilt and a new hope born of forgiveness.[3]

Viewed according to this perspective, the new philosophy-theology of hope presented itself as a strategy against oppression, and as advocate for the creation of a new possibility. But the new possibility was sought from within "the true origin" of things. It was as though recent events had been demonic deviations from civilization's true pathway forward. And the way out of oppression was to be facilitated not by the discovery of something totally new but through *renewal*, that is, the creation of a new set of circumstances in keeping with the true origin. The form of oppression being challenged was corporate rather than individual. All of humankind was depicted as being locked into oppression. Those seeking a firm basis for hope wanted to be able to announce that there was a way out. Oppression need not persist forever. There is deliverance. Bondage is not a *fait accompli*. There is hope of an exodus from bondage. Human aspirations were receptive to such announcements. Biblical exegesis supported them. Perhaps, most significant of all, the appropriate thoughts, ideas, and images had become available so that the devotee could conceive, imagine, and picture the new outlook for himself. Sustaining conceptions could be reconciled and blended with deep felt aspirations. Persons were both conscious and unconscious of a desire to be hopeful, and there were proper conceptual sanctions, justification, and verifications of that desire. Not only did persons learn to hope, but they were told, forcefully and convincingly, that it was appropriate for them to relate to their experiences this way. They hoped, and they learned and knew that hoping was the thing to do.

There were announcements of other proportions, the sort one finds when something large has occurred, and its originators are not yet aware of its respective strengths and limitations. The new denouement appeared to be so promising at first that possibility—or perhaps the condition of possibility—tended to regulate all things, sometimes even human sanity. When possibility regulates, promise creates its own world. The future is open, and the sky is the limit. Interest is directed toward prospects and strategies for realizing the future and filling the sky with benevolent forces. There is much talk about creating a more humane world, about designing the future, about the influence man's dreams have upon the configuration of things within which he lives. Bloch was heard to say that people should take daydreams seriously. Advocates of hope were overheard saying that the future isn't just anybody's future, but it belongs to someone. Indeed, the future is the product of a prior dream, an intriguing fantasy, or an imaginative plan. Finally, it seemed, Ludwig Feuerbach was being taken seriously, positively not pejoratively; and the future he detected was being filled in with the most important and attractive antidotes to human want. It was a new world, an open world, and it was more fit for the artist than for the analyst or technician. Or, indeed, if analysts and technicians were to survive, they had to lend artistry to analysis and technology. It was a world that would have to be created before it could be conceived. It was Heraclitus' world, but in Christian translation. This was its spirit, and that spirit was its driving, constructive force. But its grandeur was un-chastened.

In an earlier day, nearer the time of gestation, we had depicted the new phenomenon in terms of the contrast between time and permanence. This is the fundamental contrast and it invokes the juxtaposition of ship to cathedral in Bloch's imagery. Permanence is aligned with the cathedral against whose force Bloch placed the ship. Unlike the

cathedral, the bastion of permanence, Bloch describes the
ship, which, in learning how to move, was equipped to
traverse change, process, and perpetual unrest. The ship is
the more fit symbol for our age, Bloch had contended,
because reality is fundamentally dynamic, not static. Truth
cannot be contained in a fortress-like structure, for all time
and eternity; neither can an edifice—not even a cathedral
edifice—summarize life. Life moves. Reality is dynamic.
Process rules. As Father Heraclitus also said, "other waters
are always flowing on." Furthermore, given the fact that
reality is dynamic and process-like, there can be no permanence or rest this side of the arrival at the harbor (the place
of destiny and identity, or home). Thus the cathedral is
only deceiving itself in even giving the impression that
reality's fundamental dynamism can be contained within
the walls of a bastion-like structure. Structures cannot resist change and movement without seeking to deny or
negate reality's fundamental, driving force.

We described the move toward hope, and forecast the
swing toward time, away from permanence. We went on
to suggest that there are two religions in Christianity, one
that is vertically ordered and the other which resonates
horizontally. We noted that the two interact with each
other throughout Christian history. Somewhat analytically,
we adjudged that the horizontal process-modelled Christianity had supplanted the vertical, permanence-dominated
Christianity of an earlier era. And because Christianity is
both moods—because Catholic Christianity requires both
forms of projection—we anticipated that the future would
witness a swing in the opposite direction. In other words,
there would be a movement from change to permanence
just as there had been an enthusiasm for change earlier,
once permanence had become nonchalant. The cathedral

lacked something the ship could supply, but the ship might yearn someday to be more like the cathedral. Time had invaded the cathedral, indeed, but the mechanisms of time would one day wish the cathedral back.

It turned out that the forecast was correct: the binary interrelationships between the two polar terms all but dictated that reorientation of aspirations would produce a successor return to the original starting point. Binary orientations act this way. If spirit is ever stressed in opposition to flesh, someone is moved to advocate flesh in opposition to spirit. When authority is stressed as qualifications of human freedom, freedom becomes reasserted as an antidote to authority. When permanence becomes exclusively normative, opponents rise up to challenge permanence with time. When horizontal projection is successfully pitted against verticality, defenders of verticality raise high-minded objections. A move in one way provokes a move in the opposite direction. Indeed, this structural dynamism is characteristic of the intrinsic relationships between all binary terms. One cannot sustain the one without implying the other, and the one and the other are always related as polar opposites. Neither hope nor the future can be made to stand alone.

One could predict that horizontal-reordering would play itself out, but, of course, one could never have anticipated the combination of theoretical and historical circumstances through which this transition would occur. Perhaps we are not able to identify these factors even now. But a shift did occur, not only logically and conceptually, but also socially, politically, religiously, and theologically. Quickly, very quickly, the primal hunches and dreams were transfigured into memory. And, irony of ironies, hope itself was nuanced into the past tense.

There is a touch of sadness—a wistfulness and implicit nostalgia—in this recognition. What happened? Were the aspirations excessive? Were the claims too grand? Did enthusiasm become self-generative? Was the instinct deceptive? Or was the entire vision doomed to disappointment? The first Christians were disappointed too, we recall, when their sustaining apocalyptic hopes weren't realized, at least not in the way in which they had expected to witness fulfillment. In a very short time, had the new advocates of hope experienced the same? What happens to hope?

In America, one of the chief stimuli—or perhaps a crushing blow—may have been the McGovern campaign, particularly following the political frustrations of 1968 and the chaos of the student revolts of 1970 and 1971. Certainly not all hopes for hope had been pinned on George McGovern, on McGovern's quest for the presidency, or even on the Democratic Party. But some of the fervor of the hope movement—a fervor cognizant that human aspirations had to be interlaced with realistic political goals and concrete political action—came to focus on the prospect that McGovern, or someone of similar political persuasion and human sensitivity, could become president of the United States. For many advocates of hope, this was a make-or-break event in a long and difficult series. Previous events within the series could be interpreted in several different ways, but this one was decisive. Before this time, there were gains as well as losses; but hope could be sustained. Prior experience didn't force the conclusion that the possibility of hope had run its course. But, with the McGovern loss, that conclusion became unmistakable. What political basis for hope could there be when the candidates who best reflected the hope-position were no longer in the running for political positions of significant national and international leadership? With the McGovern loss, hope became diffused. And in becoming diffused, it also lost its corporate energy. It is too much to say that hope died in November 1972. But in a political sense, hope's future became clouded and murky, to say the least. There could be small gains here and there, but not for a long time would political realities permit the institutionalization of cherished hope motifs. We say this while recognizing that the Mc-Govern debacle may have been more symptom than act.

One finds another sort of analysis of the situation when turning to the writers of the theological treatises themselves. It is very significant that Jürgen Moltmann, the thinker upon whose conceptions of the situation many hope-advocates depended, turned to other topics. This is not to suggest that he turned away from hope. No, as he depicted it, his more recent writings are variations on the same theme, but in a more fundamental key. Thus, following hope—which was elucidated through treatises on play, planning, and liberation—Moltmann began writing more and more about the crucifixion. When he came to New York for the grand hope conference in 1971[5]—the event which some hoped would lead to a consolidation of forces between hope thinkers, process philosophers, and advocates of the position of Teilhard de Chardin—Moltmann became very upset with the heavy idle talk about theories, concepts, theoretical categories, thought patterns, and the like. Rather dramatically, he sought to switch attention to the actual conditions of poor, hungry, outcast, and significantly, oppressed, displaced, and disestablished persons. Once again, we note that his was not an attempt simply to redesign theological thought patterns, but to return to "the true origins" of things to bring about genuine renewal and an actual redressing of obligations. Within the same context, he referred to the sufferings within the world, noting that while it is appropriate for Christians to conceive of God's passion story (i.e., the crucifixion and resurrection of Jesus Christ) Christians don't think frequently or enough about "the suffering of God in the Passion Story of the world."[6]

It was as though there was no use in talking about the future, process, or hope unless one also talks about suffering. And, as he went on to say—then also on to write—one cannot understand hope unless one appreciates the need for crucifixion. Outside of crucifixion there is no hope. No matter how detailed and elaborate the plans, how fundamental the aspirations, regardless of the size or intensity of the resolve, and no matter how clever or perfect the strategy: there is no basis for hope except through the crucifixion. The crucifixion testifies that a certain man—an aspiring, hopeful man—suffered death on behalf of hope. As it was for him, so it will always be: no hope except through suffering and crucifixion. Could it be that the proper model of personality formation for those who hope is that of the martyr? Witness the succession of modern-day martyrs: John F. Kennedy, Martin Luther King, Jr., Malcolm X, Robert F. Kennedy, all within less than a ten year span. Where have all the heroes gone? Hopes are not sustained unless something dies, even when it appears that hope has died.

Was it because disciples of hope hadn't lived deeply enough that they encountered disappointment? Or had hope's currents run so deeply that they touched their truer origins, there somewhere close to the center of the human spirit? Was disappointment the indication that hope enthusiasts had come to terms with the deep ambivalence of human nature? Does the more obvious hopefulness distort one's concept of reality? And was George McGovern—and the aspirations assigned to him and other would-be champions—a victim of the distortion process? Had simple, straight-line-forward hope expected too much? Was the disposition destined for disappointment? Could it have been any other way? Can hope ever serve as the central principle in either political, social, religious, theological, or conceptual organization? Can there be *sola spes*?

It seems apparent in retrospect that the initial enthusiasm for hope was doomed to diminishment. A sign of this transposition is that scholars are already talking about the history of the theology of hope.[7] In part, attitudes to the hope movement have already assumed the past tense. True, the movement made an impact; it informed an era; but, for some, the era has passed, and its theological statements have taken on the appearance of a "period piece." Moltmann, Bloch, Metz, Pannenberg, Braaten, and the others remain unusually insightful, intriguing, and resourceful, for in each of their quivers there is a variety of arrows. Furthermore, each of the representative spokesmen are alert to the developments we have chronicled. For this reason, the theology of hope—or extensions thereof—will continue to inspire. It will continue to serve as an important source of rejuvenation. It will continue to provide interesting and arresting examples. It will always stand as the theological high-water mark of the 1960s, and Moltmann will sustain his place as the most influential Christian theologian of the era. These are irrefutable indications of high achievement, large utility, deep sensitivity, and impressive representational capacity. Most significant of all, because of the theology of hope, Christian intellectual understanding will never be able to violate a commitment to the reality of change. Theology, following hope, will always be theology of change, even when marked by concerted attempts to recapture permanence. And yet the theology of hope was designed for specific conditions. It fit those conditions, that time, and that era appropriately and immensely resourcefully. But the conditions have been altered, and, in the process, we have learned something more about the disposition's deficiencies. So, the beat must go on. Jack be nimble, Jack be quick! This is the way things go, Jack, even before your ship has come to harbor.

NOTES

1. Ihad Hassan, "Preface," in *Liberations. New Essays on the Humanities in Revolution,* ed. Ihab Hassan (Middletown: Wesleyan University Press, 1971), p. 97.

2. Ernst Bloch, *Das Prinzip Hoffnung,* 3 vols. (Frankfurt: Suhrkamp Verlag, 1959).

3. Dietrich Bonhoeffer, *The Letters and Papers from Prison,* ed. Eberhard Bethge, trans. Reginald H. Fuller (New York: Macmillan, 1953).

4. Jürgen Moltmann, "Foreword" to M. Douglas Meeks, *Origins of the Theology of Hope* (Philadelphia: Fortress Press, 1974), pp. x–xii.

5. The record of the 1971 conference has been published: Ewert H. Cousins, *Hope and the Future of Man* (Philadelphia: Fortress Press, 1972). Moltmann's contributions are included as "Response to the Opening Presentations" and "Hope and the Biomedical Future of Man."

6. Moltmann, "Response," ibid., p. 59.

7. Meeks' excellent book, *Origins of the Theology of Hope,* which is both genetic account as well as history, is the prime case in point.

PART TWO

PROVISIONS

CHAPTER FOUR

THE DYNAMICS OF POSITIVE DISENGAGEMENT

If my own sense of what is happening in the modern world is correct, then it is quite possible that we may yet see more dramatic reversals of the process of secularization. As we watch the stage of everyday life in the modern world, the action often seems to take place on one level only. The "official" reality experts deny the rumblings that may be heard from underneath—if necessary, they will sit on the trapdoor to make sure that nothing can come up from the ominous cellar. My hunch is that their effort will fail: The gods are very old and very powerful.

—Peter L. Berger[1]

In previous chapters we chronicled certain shifts in contemporary religious consciousness. We traced these shifts to alternations in crucial binary religious sets. We shall follow the same procedure in this chapter, identifying a strong religious current that has come to light more recently than either hope theology or protean-manship. This newer current also involves an alternation of contraries. On good authority, we shall refer to the disposition as *positive disengagement*, a phrase I first heard used by James E. Dittes, Yale psychologist of religion.[2] It is disengagement because it seeks a withdrawal or release from previous engagement, commitments, and overcommitment. And it is positive, rather than negative, because it seeks to disengage from involvements, commitments, and overextensions in a way which will allow the disengager to affirm the propriety of his withdrawal.

51

There are many ways of gaining access to this disposition. One of them is to recognize that many of the religious and theological tendencies of the decade from Vatican Council II forward, viewed from this perspective, can be classified as strategies of change. The theology of hope, for example, is a theological movement which attempted to organize and systematize the chief tenets of the Christian faith by making change (or process) normative. Similarly, the protean model of personality formation is devoted to change; protean man is a self-concept in motion—a self that is so fluid and flexible that enduring permanence is absent. Strategies of change are widely implicit elsewhere too. Process theology, for example, invests in change. Change has influenced the new morality. It conditions revised conceptions of religious vows. It even informs perceptions of psychological health as well as the meaning of ego strength in our time. Awareness of change compels persons to find identity in flexibility and process. Change possesses this force because reality is conceived as being dynamic and in process. There is widespread recognition that the world does not come to us set, prefixed, or already formed. As George A. Lindbeck attested during one of the earliest conferences on hope, following Vatican Council II, in 1965:

We no longer share the assumption of 400 years ago that the basic structures of the physical world, of human life and of religious existence have been and always will be much the same until the end of time. The world of human beings is changing with ever-accelerating rapidity, not as a matter of sheer flux, but in a definite direction whose final end is both fascinating and terrifying, for it seems to offer the possibility of unimaginable achievements and unimaginable disasters, and is in any case beyond the possibility of empirical prediction.[3]

He went on:

The religious implications of this are immense. Put overly simply, that which transcends the reality which we experience and know is no longer thought of (as it was in a two-story, non-historical universe) as a realm of timeless truth, value and being above us (or, where the immanence of the divine is emphasized, within and at the ground of being) which supplies the permanently stable structures of life. Rather, that which transcends the world of our experience lies ahead, in the undecipherable possibilities for good and evil into which we find ourselves hurled with ever-increasing speed. Our contemporaries are not likely to encounter transcendence as something discontinues with the world, as something which is to be entered by escaping out of time into eternity. Rather, they meet it as the future which is continuous, yet radically different, from our present world; they encounter it within the reality of their experience as the anticipations or projections of the coming world.[4]

All of this was a comment on an earlier point regarding the pervasiveness of process:

Much more important than mere temporal duration, however, is that we picture the world as a unified, developing process in which the past is not at all like the present, nor the present like the future.[5]

Strategies of change were thus designed to fit life's intrinsic structures.

But, in a very short while, the tables have been turned. Now it appears that positive disengagement is a strategy of extrication from the entanglements of the dynamics of change. The instant attractiveness of the new mood indicates that change has become too difficult to handle. Its great vitality possesses devastating force. Attempts to bring it under control often leave the subject under its control. Change is rugged and powerful. It transforms everything it touches. It rearranges boundaries. It upsets preestablished order. It modifies relationships. It alters contours. It reallocates and redistributes resources. It creates new shapes, and inserts qualifications into definitions. Not content with simple composition, it decomposes, then recomposes. It modulates, transposes, transfigures, and diversifies. It produces instant obsolescence. It makes early retirement mandatory. It obliges persons sensitive to its dictates not merely "to be" but rather "to cope." Being is changing, and becoming is coping. Coping means striving. Striving means contending. And contending implies struggle. Not always successful.

The religious life knows something, too, of the plusses and minuses of change. Change is opportunity; it is also temptation. It provides the occasion for human freedom, but, sometimes, at the price of an accelerated loss of personal centeredness. Sensitivity to change enables one to swing with life, but it also antagonizes one's sense of permanence. Involvements in change-producing ventures makes one manifestly *au courant*, but it can also leave one frenzied emotionally and bereft spiritually. Identification with consciousness-changing enterprises places one at the cutting edge, but the rest of life isn't able always to catch up. Eventually change creates the need to rearrange all of life's patterns, and some of these patterns cannot be tinkered with that easily. Gains here are losses there. Resolutions here are new questions there. Some things are made new by change; other things cannot survive change. Change creates delights; it also spells suffering. Its achievements are always twofold.

There have been dedicated proponents of the theology of hope, for instance, who have found that the forces of time and change were destructive and disorienting, as well as being beneficial and catalytic. One assumes the disposition at a high cost. And perhaps it will be some time before we know whether the challenges of change require more than the human spirit is equipped to give. Does change become difficult because human inertia resists its demands? Or are there limits to flexibility beyond which one dare not go?

For whatever reasons, there are many earlier enthusiasts who want now to back off. At the same time, they are sufficiently in touch with things to want to resist withdrawal and/or resignation. It must be coping rather than copping out. Sheer withdrawal simply will not do. The former positive engager wants to become disengaged, but positively, not negatively. He seeks disengagement in a form which will confirm his own positive motivation. He doesn't want to turn away from change, and yet he realizes that its forces are larger than he can control. He cannot control it. Within its power, he loses his own control. Thus disengagement is not a debunking of change, and not simply a reversal of enthusiasms cherished a short while ago. But it is an attempt to find the resourcefulness to rediscover a certain singleness-of-mind—a singleness-of-mind in disengagement not unlike the singleness that had been devoted to strategies of change.

In confessional terms, disengagement may take a variety of forms: "I thought what I was doing before was right, but, before long, I discovered that I was being exploited. Perhaps I was only deceiving myself. Now, I'm dropping out for awhile, dropping out by stepping back, perhaps only for awhile, to gather myself together." Or it may be expressed this way: "I believed in what I was doing, and it was right at the time. But it isn't right any longer. The ground rules seem to have shifted. So I am seeking release. Through no other way can I hope to move forward." Or it can be the simple statement, "I knew what I was doing when I was doing it, and it is still necessary to do. But I've worn myself out and need to take a rest, at least for awhile."

Personal encounters with change often found dramatic expression. But there are other signs too, less serious signs, perhaps, that positive disengagement is all around us. One can cite the nostalgia tendency of the present time as a similar case in point. We refer to the attempt to recover whatever situation was there prior to the onset of the frenzy, the yearning for a time of quiet and romantic tranquility. Nostalgia for the music of an earlier day, for older fashions and styles of dress, indeed, even for the village store, the college, the city square, the English cottage, the Model A (or Model T) Ford, with the rumble seat. All of this testifies to the expansiveness of the mood. University life has seen the recurrence of the sock hop. There is a new enthusiasm for fraternities and sororities. Even in elementary schools, children celebrate by donning clothes from an earlier era. *American Graffiti* may well have become the first of a series of filmed portrayals of the nostalgia mood. The disposition is strong. It is real. It is present. Possibly there is disengagement because the modern era has become too complex, too complicated, too large, too multiform, too full of problems, too cluttered. Positive disengagement seeks a new, viable form of simplicity. And there is a hint that the same can be found by stepping, turning, or reaching back.

The examples build upon themselves. The distinguished American historian, Page Smith, wrote recently about the wealth of books one finds in the bookstores these days. His point, of course, was that no more books need be written for awhile. Books are hard on trees, and, besides, more books are written than the eye can scan or the human mind absorb. But the sub-point was the interesting one. The great proportion of books now on the market and on bookstore tables are of the "how-to-do-it" variety. Such books

provide instructional guides—maps, plans, sketches, and designs—not only for building kitchen cabinets, learning to use
the typewriter, or repairing automobiles and television sets.
In addition, they deal with such primary human functions
as how to sleep, how to eat, how to rest, how to enjoy sexual
relationships, how to conquer boredom, how to walk, jog,
run, keep fit, breathe, meditate, find happiness, etc. From
this amazing array, one begins to suspect that human beings
have lost their grip on the most basic human functions. The
most fundamental human processes seem to lie beyond our
present capacities. It appears that human beings need to
re-learn the most elemental facts of life. Smith writes: "It
is as though the simplest human functions and relationships
had somehow been forgotten."[6]

This is part of the background of the strategy of positive
disengagement. Life has become too full, too complex, too
difficult to manage. The social and political commitments
have been too demanding. The results have been dis-
appointing, to say the least, for basic, fundamental human
simplicity has gotten lost. Unless there is simplicity, there
is no hope for singleness-of-mind. And, as we have been
arguing, unless there is the prospect for singleness-of-mind,
it is difficult to find a reliable base for religion.

As indicated, I am indebted to Dittes for the language I
am using here. The phrase "positive disengagement" is his;
it is his before it can be possessed, repossessed, and restyled
by anyone else. In his own development of this theme, he
takes issue with Kenneth Keniston, the author of the book,
The Uncommitted.[7] In that book, Keniston has identified a
certain malaise among young people which he depicts as
being a desire for commitment coupled with a sense that
there is nothing worthy of such large, unqualified commitment. That is, in Keniston's view, young people have both

the capacity and the desire for commitment. But there is nothing toward which commitment can be directed. There is nothing forceful or compelling enough. Nothing large enough. Nothing interesting enough. Nothing sustaining enough. Consequently, in Keniston's view, the capacity and desire for commitment falters. The propensity is there, but young people remain uncommitted.

Dittes sees it in another way. Instead of interpreting the situation in terms of lack of commitment because there is nothing worthy of commitment, Dittes perceives a deliberate dedication toward uncommitment. Perhaps it would be more accurate to refer to the disposition as "a-commitment." Young people are committed toward being uncommitted. Thus they are intent on exercising disengagement. Disengagement fashions itself as uncommitment, but not because commitment has gone by default. Rather, the young person's desire and strategy is to separate himself from commitments that are conflicting, complicating, debilitating, and thus prevent the individual from exercising singleness-of-mind.

The old Tillichian ploys can't work very well in this situation. One cannot presume that everyone is committed to some mastering or controlling life-principle, and the trick comes in knowing which of the several competing principles is worthy of one's ultimate concern. Neither can one take the prospect as self-evident that everyone is disposed to ultimacy of some sort, and variety pertains only to its identification. No, the new disposition jars Tillichian categories. The best the latter can do is to register the former as ultimate unconcern. But this is awkward interpretation at best. The straining of categories illustrates that it won't do nowadays to say (as some have paraphrased the words of Martin Luther) that everyone worships someone or something, but the real task is to locate the God who is worthy of man's devotion and trust. Nor is it possible to disclose an implicit theism in ultimate unconcern, for—unlike the interchangeability of ultimate concern and concern for the ultimate in original formulation—ultimate unconcern cannot be translated into unconcern for the ultimate. The tables have been turned. The new situation is more complicated.

But, while typifying a new mood, positive disengagement possesses direct lines of continuity with ancient and classical mystical traditions. The one flows into the other. The latter can be the way the former is expressed. Disengagement assumes form in mystical awareness. Indeed, one of the ways of locating and interpreting positive disengagement religiously is to see it as deliberate withdrawal from a temporal, conflicted world. For the mystic withdrawal accompanies a process of introversion through which the self seeks to establish and enjoy consciousness of reality's deeper levels and fuller dimensions. Mystics occasionally refer to this process as "a stilling of the surface mind" and as "a journey toward the center." Thus the mystic's efforts at disengagement can be referred to in positive terms too. They intend not simply to deny the existence of the disparate world, but, instead, to identify a standpoint from which one can affirm reality positively. Through the centuries mystical awareness has provided documentation that disengagement is a frequent precondition to positive affirmation.

Before he is anything else, the mystic is one who knows the necessity of a discriminating sense of life. He perceives that reality is multidimensional, and that its various layers or regions are not of equal worth. He senses too that not all places and times enjoy the same status. His intention is to establish the basis for singleness-of-heart. Without the possibility of a personal singleness, there is no way to place the self under a mastering principle. As Søren Kierkegaard said, "purity of heart is to will one thing." The mystic seeks singleness too. Indeed, mystical experience is a way of lending singleness comprehensively to human life. And yet singleness can never be achieved at the price of a lost or qualified multidimensionality. Singleness-of-heart in a multidimensional world is the mystic's goal. It may well be the religious goal of every sensitive, self-conscious person. But singleness cannot be found if the self has become lost in disparateness, if it wallows in conflict, without some reliable form of stability. A self spread out in disparateness runs the risk of forfeiting its capacity for centeredness.

This must be the reason the mystic is so often criticized as being "other-worldly." It also must be the reason the mystic has recourse, so frequently, to language within which words like "transcendence" register. The world of disparateness—the world of "the most obvious"—holds so many threats and risks to religious sensitivity. Because the chance that the self will get lost there is high, there are built-in cautions against investing too much of oneself in the world of here-and-now.

Thus the mystic has always felt a certain aversion toward the world of process and change, sensing, as Plato aptly put it, that the temporal world passes away while the world of permanence abides. Permanence is usually located transcendentally, to indicate that the "other world"—the true world—isn't qualified or infected by the disparateness, sameness, and pervasive homogeneity. For when the here-and-now world is taken as being the only world, or the only normative context of orientation, the mystic senses that the conditions for establishing an authentic and sustaining center for the self are qualified or absent. The mystic feels compelled to counter that the transcendent world, by contrast, is the real world, and the contemplative life (*vita contemplativa*) offers definite steps to reach that world. But it requires disengagement—indeed, a disengagement that is freeing, not guilt binding. This is the gist of mystical positive disengagement. And it is very close in spirit to the variety of religious expressions which have followed a recognition that the self has over-invested in socio-political programs of a marked "this-worldly" character.

It is significant, too, that the advent of the new mysticism follows directly upon the heels of disappointment regarding the theologies of change and process. Some will add that mysticism became attractive following a time of recognized overcommitment to strategies for coping with change. When change becomes too cumbersome, and when process brings lack of personal resolve and an inability to know where one stands, mysticism is standing by as a veritable and perpetual open space. But it isn't a rest home. It needn't serve simply as a means of escape. It isn't just a strategy of rescue from situations *homo religiosus* cannot tolerate. Instead, it has its own positive dynamism. It provides a religious resourcefulness that the various theologies of change and process are unable to articulate and, perhaps, to fathom. We have mentioned this capacity for transcendence and its mechanism for disengagement. Not to be overlooked are its propensity for inspiring quiet, its facilitation of introspection, its corrective powers with regard to the distortions which accompany indiscriminate immersion in "the most obvious world," not to mention the implicit discipline it provides. Ironically, these are strategies for coping with change. Mysticism copes with change by giving its place, but not in every place. Mysticism cultivates a vantage point from which to give change a relative and subordinate place. For this reason, mysticism is more than a device for coping with incidental malevolent side effects of overcommitment to change and process. More profoundly, it has been—and continues to be—the primary religious vehicle through which positive disengagement is both exercised and expressed. Mysticism is compatible with positive disengagement. In addition, a mysticism that is properly grounded and deftly executed illustrates that disengagement can be positive.

I shall cite a specific example, for it supports this chapter's theme and provides a lucid preview of things to come. I had occasion recently to teach a course of medieval Christian thought. Because of nearly a decade of lack of interest in the subject, together with a number of local circumstances, the course was being offered for the first time in several years. The class consisted of a number of very good students—some majors in medieval studies, an equal number from religious studies, and a group of students who had had no previous experience in either subject, thus, certainly, little or no acquaintance with medieval thought. It was a good class, for the students and instructor worked together throughout the quarter, almost as if all of us were encountering the subject for the first time.

Along the way one of the students confessed that he had discovered within himself a certain monastic bent. He had had inklings of this tendency before, but through concentrated reading in medieval contemplative literature it had been brought to a sharper conscious awareness. Wondering what to do to pursue the interest further, he became interested in visiting monasteries in the area surrounding Santa Barbara. And before the class had finished there were several others in similar situations, interested in the monastic life, not only for scholarly reasons, but more immediately, personally. On at least two occasions a dozen students or more made an attempt to become better acquainted with the dynamics of monastic life by visiting available centers in the immediate geographical area.

As a final event in the sequence of visits, the group organized a "field trip" to the Monastery of the Poor Clares in Santa Barbara. I shall recount the sequence of events because it bears upon the theme of this chapter. The group was met at the door of the convent by one of the novice-sisters. We learned later that two or three of the sisters are referred to as externs; that is, nuns who are designated by the others to carry on public responsibilities. This includes answering the door and telephone, carrying on business with persons who come to the door, meeting whomever is "public," etc. It is a liaison position, for the entire monastery itself is cloistered.

Our "guide" ushered us into a small visiting room, meticulously clean, polished, economical, and manifestly unluxurious. The door closed behind us. We sat on chairs in the room by ourselves, trying, if only by being quiet, to be duly reverent. No one else was present in the room for approximately eight to ten minutes. Because our chairs were placed against the four walls of the room, we sat facing each other. This prompted us to ask ourselves if the chairs shouldn't be moved so that our orientation to the room would be more proper. "Shouldn't we all be facing in the same direction?" someone asked. Sensing consensus, we speculated as to the direction in which we should be facing. There was a crucifix in the room, atop a table of sorts, but it didn't appear as if the table were an altar. Immediately opposite the table with the crucifix, across the room, was a window; or, at least, it appeared to be a window, for a shade had been pulled down over it—perhaps, we wondered, to shelter the room from the bright early afternoon sunlight? Should we be facing eastward? And as we sat there offering suggestions to each other about the direction in which we should be facing, the sort of demeanor that seemed expected of us, the shade was lifted. Instead of its covering a window, it guarded an opening to an adjacent room. Through the opening, no longer covered by the shade, we could see approximately ten to twelve nuns, sitting in habits, on institutional straight-back chairs. They had entered the adjoining room so quietly—or perhaps they were there all the time—that we had had no awareness that they were there. We could see them in the other room, through the opening in the wall which, formerly, had been covered by the shade. But the opening was protected by a formidable metal grating. It looked like ticket windows I remembered from my boyhood, like the old-fashioned teller stations in banks, or the stamp windows in the post offices of some years ago, or the ticket offices in railroad stations along the main line of the Union Pacific Railroad in western Nebraska, all of this before the metal criss-crossed grating was eliminated or replaced by glass. We introduced ourselves to one another, through the "window" protected by the metal grating. Despite this large physical barrier, we were urged to establish our relationship on a first name basis. Then the questions and the dialogue began. All of the questions were ours; none were tendered from the other side.

"Tell us something about how you spend your time each day," one of the students asked. It seemed like an appropriate opener, but it provoked laughter, even before the student finished asking it. The answer was that there is no typical day in the convent. Each day is different; and each one contains surprises and unexpected events. This was the answer to the question, but not the explanation for the laughter—a laughter that was recurrent throughout the conversation. The day is regulated by the canonical calendar, a calendar that is prescribed by the Order. The daily routine was described to us in some detail, from the earliest morning hours, through the early evening's bedtime, including the first prayer watch at midnight each new day.

"Was it hard for you personally to leave your family when you came to make vows to enter the community?" There was unanimity in the answer. Most of the nuns had felt very close to their families. Most continue to feel this closeness, even though miles and years have erected additional barriers. Most continue to feel the pains of separation even though, for many, the act of separation occurred many years ago. For most, it was only through suffered wrenching that "leaving home" was possible in the first place. One of the older nuns confessed that she had chosen Santa Barbara because of its proximity to the San Andreas fault. She reasoned that if the monastery were destroyed by an earthquake, she would feel less obligation to stay. The earthquake would be a token sign that she could return to her family, the providence of God confirming.

"If I were a member of the community here, would I be allowed to keep my portable radio?" one of the students asked. "No, but we do listen to music and play recordings. It isn't quiet all the time." (More corporate convent mirth.)

Then, "How does it happen that you seem to know so much about what is going on in the world outside, even though you hardly ever move beyond the walls of the monastery?" (The nuns told us that they had been out of the convent earlier that week, en masse, to vote in a California primary election.) "Do you read newspapers and watch the news on television?" (Again, laughter.) It was as if the nuns sensed that the inquirer was trying to find

65

access—both for himself, and, perhaps, on their behalf too—
to a world that was utterly remote. What would life be if
one were cloistered? Certainly, one would come close to
the fellow members of the cloistered community, and one
would no doubt come to a deeper self-consciousness than
is possible elsewhere. Cloistering should be able to further
these goals; it should be reliable in this respect. The combination of closeness to a small select group of persons, all
more or less like-minded, all of the same sex, all living for
the same expressed purposes, together with separation from
persons not like-minded, not of the same sex, and motivated
by a wide range of expressed and tacit purposes, this combination ought to promote the gathering of the self. It
ought to facilitate introversion. It should assist one in
coming to terms with the rhythms and dynamisms of his
innermost self. In Friedrich Schleiermacher's language,
cloistered life should support "the abiding in the self." But
what does it say about life outside the cloistered walls?
What about the externalized self? What about the world
that can never be persuaded to be like-minded? What
about "that other" vast range of things? Is there any real
vital feel for that world, for the here-and-now world?

The sisters understood the question. It was clear that
they had wrestled with it more than once. It was a question that had to be settled each day if cloistered monastic
life were to remain a vital, personal, and corporate option.
"Yes," came the answer, "we have newspapers and other
reading materials." The *Christian Science Monitor* was a
paper the nuns took seriously; they were not as well pleased
with the *National Catholic Reporter*. But they did not
watch television. They didn't own one; they didn't want
one. Some of the nuns who had been in the monastery for
a long time confessed that they had seen television only

once or twice, and never watched it except when some large, extremely significant historical event, like a moon landing by American astronauts, was being televised. Some of the younger nuns, who had experienced television before entering the convent, prior to the taking of vows, said that they found more entertainment in watching their older sisters watch television than in watching television themselves.

But the answer to the questions seemed less serious than the questions. The students persisted. Such determined inquisitiveness made evasiveness intolerable. "How do you keep in touch with things outside?" This time the answer was more subtle. "We know what is going on in the world because we are near the center, day by day, hour by hour. Our life is hid with Christ's in God. God is at the center. God is the center. And through our life with God, through Christ, we are present at the center too. If anything happens at the periphery it must somehow reflect back upon the center. When it does we know about it. And much that happens at the edges has radiated originally from the center. Nothing can occur anywhere in the world that is detached from the center. If one abides in the center, at the 'still-point,' he is also present everywhere else."

This is what the students had wanted to find out. This testimony described a disengagement from the world which enabled one to take one's proper place at the world's center. It was a move away from the periphery in favor of the center so that life at the periphery could be properly centered. It was calculated withdrawal so that the relation of center to periphery could be focussed and ordered. Moving away from the world was necessary to be in the world in a more profound way. Disengagement was required so that the world could be established, for, as Mircea Eliade, has taught us, centering itself is a metaphor of creation.[8]

The nuns recognize that not everyone is called to this way of life. They are quick to acknowledge, too, that monasticism is not the only way to enunciate the Christian gospel or to give expression to the religious life. Monasticism is not for everyone. The cloistered life will always be a minority option at most, for a selected few. The nuns are aware of this. And yet, in their view, monasticism is responsive to a deep qualitative dimension of reality. Finding "value" in this way of life should not lead us to expect that the nuns will defend their orientation on pragmatic grounds alone. They are aware of the suspicions, charges, and criticisms that have been directed toward monasticism in the modern world:

Is the challenging cry of the conciliar age, "Come down from your ivory tower; involve yourself!" addressed to contemplative religious? In its broader and nobler sense of abandoning, selfishness and a certain, snobbish, spiritual eclecticism, definitely, yes. In its superficial, and sadly more common, sense of abandoning the cloister and all it implies, no. For the "tower" of the true contemplative is God Himself, from whom she may in no wise detach herself if she would remain faithful to the sublime office given her by Holy Church.[9]

And they recognize that they have been influenced by the same deceptive pragmatic criteria in seeking sanction for their style of life.

But we have been unmistakably tainted by the activist, materialism of our day. We fear to lose face in a society feverish with "doing" and forgetful of "being."

This has prompted them, on occasion, to defend the cloister in current pragmatic "service" terms:

When we have proved to our satisfaction that monks and nuns are actively serving mankind, though in a silent and invisible way, we feel that their way of life, and our sympathy with it, are properly vindicated.

But the real "reasons" for their way of life are more fundamental. It speaks of detachment, singularity, in a majestically disengaged manner:

The "Why?" of cloistered contemplative life is answered, then, by the supreme majesty of Almighty God. . . . It is the poignant "Why?" of a costly perfume charging the air with spice and tears as it spilled unmeasured, over the feet of Christ. It is the lyric "Why?" of ". . . the solitary flower of the mountains, far up at the fringe of eternal snows, that has never been looked upon by the eye of man; . . . the unapproachable beauty of the poles and the deserts of the earth, that remain forever useless for the service and the purposes of man . . ."

This is withdrawal and initiation at the same time. It is intended as disengagement from the world in a positive, formative, and creative sense.

The students found the nuns' report compelling. Some of them said that they wanted to return to the monastery from time to time, perhaps to worship, perhaps for counsel, perhaps to keep today's awareness alive. Others talked about the need to establish centers for spiritual growth so that those persons who cannot make life-long vows can at least come to refresh and center themselves from time to time through temporary exposure to the monastic life. The students' interest in the monastic way of life, in short, was only sustained by the testimony of the Sisters of Poor Clare.

In the discussion following, many of the same students admitted that they had not been going to church recently. They didn't want to go; in fact, they felt no need to go. Nor did they feel guilty—as one time they had—about not going. The reason seemed to be that in their minds the church no longer concerned itself with religion. Surely, it was "relevant" and it promoted "commitment" and "involvement." Furthermore, the church was engaged in many important and necessary issues and ventures. But one cannot find religion there. In fact, the students tended to agree that if one were upset by a burning religious question, or if he sought counsel regarding the formation of the religious life, he shouldn't expect to find insight or illumination from within the church. In some of their minds, the church was being motivated by something else. And the same large and proper engagements foreclose recognition of deeper religious consequences. The students, too, were searching for a mystery that can be trusted, sensing all the while that it is nothing other than mystery, that mysteries cannot be translated into something else.

Ironically, the fact that positive disengagement is resisted by present church priorities is taken as a sign by many that the church is conducting its affairs properly. According to this attitude, disengagement's inaccessibility indicates that the churches are properly challenging society's status quo. This implies that churches are taking their most recent obligations seriously: to be present where reality flows, to assist making certain that life be kept moving, flexible, and free. This was the mood of the middle and late 1960s, a mood that has remained dominant in some quarters even to the present time. To advocates of engagement and involvement, disengagement presents itself as an atavistic stance. It is a return to a position that was rendered obsolete by clear recognition and sober assessment of the actual condition of the world today. After all, the burning political dilemmas are still with us. Recalcitrant social inequities have not yet been redressed. Oppressed persons remain in bondage. An increasingly large portion of the world's population is undernourished, and, in an alarming and appalling number of cases, simply starving. Disfavored peoples have not been liberated. Minority persons and third-world nations continue to be discriminated against. Energy is running low. Pollution is running high. The nuclear arms race continues unabated. A food crisis is imminent. Political leadership has been corrupted. The goals of positive futuristic philosophies have not been achieved, and seem more distant now than when they were first announced. Humankind's most persistent foes seem to have found a new resourcefulness. They have not been conquered. How can one talk of disengagement in the face of all this? How can disengagement be positive? How can it be given religious sanction? How can it be offered as having a distinctive religious value? Given the depth, immensity, and acuteness of the world's manifold problems, can disengagement be anything other than irresponsibility? Isn't disengagement overt disacceptance of one's innate human obligations? If for no other reason than human sensitivity or sympathy, can disengagement ever be condoned? In this context, isn't disengagement a repudiation of one's own inner moral sense? This is the critique, and it has been registered forcefully and eloquently in our time.

In some sense, both sides are correct, of course. They are correct not because each has hold of a piece of the truth, but, more profoundly, because the two are expressing polar sides of an important contrary. The Poor Clares would have a difficult time condoning the cloister if, instead of giving life a center, its function were strictly diversionary. Centering implies dynamic action, which means perpetual motion back and forth from the periphery to the core. But how are centers and peripheral points fixed? How does one determine which is which? Isn't it necessary to locate— or fix—a center before there can be a periphery? And can't one person's center be another person's periphery? Can one engage the center and disengage the periphery? Or, is the periphery to be engaged by disengaging the center? Does the center remain center if one abides there all the time? Does a previous center—now disengaged—become an instant periphery? Can there be a disengaged center? And isn't there a center—or at least a centering process—that is placed at the edges? When one reaches "the edges of history" (to use William Irwin Thompson's phrase),[10] for example, has he departed from the center or come closer to it?

There is another important dimension to the story which needs to be identified, that is, the dimension of pilgrimage: pilgrimage as a means of enlightenment, and enlightenment as an instrument of disengagement. The class had undertaken a pilgrimage. It had given itself—in brief, abbreviated, and temporary form—to a venture not unlike pilgrimages that have been recurring in the world for a significant length of time. Pilgrimage is the proper name for it. Because of the nature of the subject we were studying, we chose to seek out Christian monasteries and convents. The Poor Clares provided a natural pilgrimage station because of their medieval origins. According to the same criterion, we could justify our interest in visiting the Franciscan Old Mission. But thousands of others recently have taken a similar interest to other sorts of convents, monasteries, and centers for spirituality. We refer not only to the Transcendental Meditation movement among young people in America, the devotion to the person and teaching of the Maharishi, to other quickly westernized Indian gurus, and to fascination with Zen monasteries, the work of the Esalen Institute, the preoccupation with humanistic psychology, and also to the less obvious forms of the same quest. All of this seems to express a concerted attempt to find the "still-point" beyond or behind confliction. And, as has always been the case, the discovery of the still-point requires a pilgrimage, or a journey in space and time.

The new fascination with native American (American Indian) culture, and, particularly, with native American religion, can be cited as a like-minded development. The journeys in space and time, the pilgrimages in self-consciousness, to locate the place and fix the time (before time) when reality had not yet been spoiled, earth had not been removed from its axis, creation was still good, fresh from its creator's hands—this is the quest for primordial simplicity. And its style is singularly disengaging. The irony is that one can defend the return to the cloister on Norman O. Brown's terms. It is a movement with which Brown could be sympathetic. The new monastic religion is not spirit vs. body religion; its strategy is not to disembody souls, but, more profoundly, to set the life of both body and spirit free by cultivating appropriate physical and spiritual processes of renewal.

The reversals implicit in the new religious temper dramatically illustrate the complexities of the current religious situation. Binarial alternation can work its wiles in a variety of ways simultaneously. For this reason, arguments for disengagement can be tapped—perhaps equally effectively—in support of engagement. Indeed, disengagement from one perspective registers as engagement in another setting. "Dis-en" and "en" depend upon one's position; they are determined by one's horizon. Thus, as in kinetic art, what one sees is where one stands; and when one's standpoint shifts, so also does the complexion of the reality he faces. Disengagement, that is to say, can be depicted in positive religious terms. Disengagement can become the means of a richer positive engagement.

NOTES

1. Peter L. Berger, "Some Second Thoughts on Substance vs. Functional Definitions of Religion," *Journal for the Scientific Study of Religion* 13, No. 2 (1974): 133.

2. James E. Dittes, "When Idols Crumble: The Art and Agony of Disengagement," Presidential Address to the Society for the Scientific Study of Religion, October 1973.

3. George A. Lindbeck, "The Framework of Catholic-Protestant Disagreement," in *The Word in History* (The St. Xavier Symposium), ed. T. Patrick Burke (New York: Sheed and Ward, 1966), p. 107.

4. Ibid.

5. Ibid.

6. Page Smith, "What This Country Really Needs Is a Moratorium on the Writing of Books," in the *Los Angeles Times* (June 28, 1974), Part II, p. 7.

7. Kenneth Keniston, *The Uncommitted. Alienated Youth in American Society* (New York: Dell Publishing Company, 1960).

8. Mircea Eliade has expressed this thought repeatedly in his writings, and in summary fashion in *The Sacred and the Profane,* trans. Willard R. Trask (New York: Harcourt, Brace, 1959), especially pp. 62–65.

9. Sister Mary of the Trinity, O.P., *Worthy is the Lord (An Explanation of Cloistered Contemplative Life),* a pamphlet distributed by the Poor Clares. All succeeding quotations regarding the cloistered religious life are taken from this pamphlet.

10. William Irwin Thompson, *At the Edge of History* (New York: Harper and Row, 1971).

CHAPTER FIVE

WISDOM FROM THE ANALYTICAL FATHERS

> Ways of making sense of the world are plural, incorrigibly
> so in our time.   Living with the revolution means living with
> that.   It does not mean abandoning our own ways of making
> sense.   —Frank Kermode[1]

This book has focussed on tension, conflict, and the place and role of contrariness in contemporary religious consciousness.   We have isolated specific instances of contrariness, and have watched points of religious orientation shift from one pole to the other.   Robert Jay Lifton draws upon a psychiatrist's perspective, for example, to document a shift from authority to id-styled freedom.   Lifton presents protean man, the dominant model of personality formation for our time, as a self-concept in motion.   Norman O. Brown, a classicist steeped in psychoanalytic theory, highlights the alternation between spirit and body in announcing that enlightened body awareness is a precondition of the full salvation persons seek.   The theology of hope, stimulated originally by awareness of the pervasiveness of change, has been effected by the transition from change back to permanence.   These were our prime examples.   Then, in the last chapter, we analyzed the way in which recent transitional action among contraries has produced or stimulated a new need for disengagement from change.   Each illustrative instance referred to a dominant form of contrariness.   In each instance, we traced dynamic interaction between two poles of contrariness.

Contrariness is all around us. It affects the way we view things. It even affects religious orientations. Indeed, if our thesis is correct, contrariness is one of the most crucial facts about the way we design and negotiate religious orientations. The past ten years has seen dramatic alternations within contrariness. But has it yet found a way beyond contrariness? Does positive disengagement lead to anything more than a perpetual oscillation between existing polar opposites?

Before we address these questions directly, we must step back aways to say something about the methodology we have employed here. We do this not to isolate methodological issues for methodological reasons, but because of an obligation to make our conceptual strategy self-conscious. Ours has been an attempt to discern the dynamic of change. Most methodologies have turned their attention the other way. They have been designed to identify normative features—that is, the normative and repeatable law-like element, the pattern, standard, essence, nature, ontological, metaphysical, or conceptual core element, etc. But the approach used in this book is designed to mark and trace processes in motion. It is conceived to enunciate dynamic factors rather than permanent, inflexible, repeatable patterns. For this reason, because of its novelty, we are obliged to enunciate some of the principles on which our approach depends.

But we do not want to claim too much. It would be inaccurate to say, for example, that there are no effective methodologies for dealing with the change factor in religion. Indeed, very impressive statistical methodologies have been designed to measure paths of deviation, alteration, variation, and change in religious attitudes and behavior. In fact some of the best sociological statistical surveys on record have been ones dealing with subjects of direct religious interest. Statistical inquiries have been particularly useful in plotting changes in religious comportment. And yet, the same statistical work—as sophisticated and rigorous as it is—has not been equipped to penetrate some of the issues we have attempted to face. The proponents of statistical methods of research, aware of the strengths and limits of their own ploy, are quick to trace, describe, and chronicle, but additional intellectual work is required to explain and interpret. Statistical evidence can be marshalled to spot and document shifts in religious orientation, but, as statistical evidence, it could not supply the theory which explains the shifts.

Usually, the next stage of analysis involves placing the results of statistical inquiry into meaningful sequences within larger frameworks. It is not enough to be able to plot this or that instance of religious change. It is necessary also to place the particular instance within a larger constellation or sequence of trends. To do this, the analyst must identify or select a more comprehensive unit of altered directionality, that is, if he believes the individual case reflects more extensive currents and tendencies. Oftentimes, the shift from the particular to the more general and comprehensive has been achieved via a theory of evolution. The assumption is that this or that particular instance of change belongs to a larger and more comprehensive process. Evolutionary theory is attractive too because it refers to a process that can be broken down into constituent chronological segments. Evolution means that the process possesses times, periods, and stages. The pathway forward is not made up of contents of one kind, but there are distinct moments and times—a veritable evolutionary calendar—which possess their own proprieties. Once these periods have been demarcated, there is a framework for mapping historical and cultural change. The framework can be employed too to plot changes in religious comportment. In each case, particular changes are correlated with transitions from one stage of evolutionary progression to the next.

For example, the classical interpretation of the relationship between myth, metaphysics, and science is based upon an evolutionary model. The same model has become prominent in historical studies, and has been employed in a wide variety of cultural analyses as well. When first conceived, the model was used to explain how it could be that reality was susceptible to successive layers or degrees of explanation. The world was apprehended mythologically first, the model attested. Then, as empirical knowledge became more extensive and rigorous, the imaginary features of mythology were transposed into metaphysical principles. Next, when the transcendental and abstract quality of metaphysical knowledge was pared down by a larger accumulation of empirical, verifiable fact, together with rigorous methods for discerning such facts, metaphysics gave way to science. So August Comte said, and since his time scores of schools of scholars have been in agreement.[2]

The myth-metaphysics-science sequence is one way of dealing with variation in change, but it is not a very adequate way of dealing with the fact of contrariness in change. In other words, when the evolutionary process moves forward directly, the myth-metaphysics-science sequence has some explanatory cogency. But when there are skips and halts, movements back and forth, occurrences followed by their own dissolution, positive steps forward creating their own negations, contrariness, conflict, opposition, antipathy, antagonism, contrariness, etc., the simple straightline-forward evolutionary model is not very satisfactory. As Raimundo Panikkar argues brilliantly, secularization is itself a kind of mythology.[3]

For example, one can place *mythos* and *logos* as being in sequence with one another. This same sequence can be correlated with the succession between the numbers one and two. The movement from mythology to metaphysics to science would involve three, not two, numbers; but it continues to be a sequential shift. There is movement between myth, metaphysics, and science as between the sequence one-two-three. Similarly, while *mythos* and *logos* are not altogether continuous, they are not completely discontinuous either. Some of the materials of *mythos* survive the transition to *logos*. Indeed, some of the content of *mythos* can be translated into *logos*. This happens because *mythos* and *logos* are both continuous and discontinuous modes of apprehension. They are not antithetical. They are dissimilar, but, as Paul Ricoeur and others have shown, they are not actually variant.[4] To deal with modes that are contrary is a different matter. It requires a different strategy. For, in the case of contrariness, the relation of one to two is both continuous, sequential, and antithetical. It is not one followed by two simply, but one followed by two while one and two are contrary. It is not one plus two simply, but one plus two and one versus two simultaneously, like this:

$$(1 + 2) + (1 \text{ vs. } 2) = \text{the structure of religious reality}$$

And this is a complicated sequence.

There is a file of interpretation on the subject, of course. The classical Hegelian model, for example, was tailor-made to sustain contrariness within evolutionary change. It is— or was—a beautiful model, remarkable and memorable both for its scope and its resilience. Though conceived more than a century ago, it continues to enjoy a prominence in various sectors of the interpretational world because of its ability to mark historical change and to lend periodicital sense to progress. When first designed, it was employed to chart and explain the evolutionary path of the all-compelling and all-controlling World Spirit (*Geist*). It pertained to the history of human consciousness. It was a way of marking corporate and spiritual growth and experience. As Hegel perceived it, the movement of the Spirit was regulated by a specific positive affirmation, followed by its contrary or negation, followed by the resolution of positive-negative in synthesis. Thesis, anti-thesis, then syn-thesis. And the resolving synthesis formed the starting point for a continuation of the sequence via thesis, antithesis, and synthesis. It was an ongoing, recurrent pattern which allowed the forward path of history to be both cyclical and progressive.

Hegel's system was made more complex by the insertion of the dynamics of concretion into the evolutionary process forward. By this insertion, the transition from spirit to concrete objectivization of spirit occurred in conjunction with the measured, sequential unfolding of thesis, antithesis, and synthesis. The movement forward was understood to be multilayered. The scheme described how contrariness could be absorbed by a uni-directional forward-tending process. The ingredients of contrariness were present, but eventually they yielded to the unifying synthesizing workings of the all-comprehensive process forward. The entire vision was enormously impressive, almost in the way that Wagnerian music is both enormous and impressive, because of its intricacies, scope, and attempted exhaustiveness.

But the Hegelian model is found wanting—despite its great resourcefulness—when it is drawn upon for insights regarding shifts and alternations within religious consciousness. For, as we have seen, the shifts within religious consciousness cannot be absorbed into the familiar pattern of thesis, antithesis, and synthesis in a recurrent pattern of evolution. Religious consciousness doesn't seem to be motivated by a progression from positive statement to negation of statement to resolution of positive and negative. Instead, religious consciousness seems to be formed by a dialectic which oscillates back and forth, almost like a pendulum swinging. The only safeguard against over-stresses and single-minded commitments is the pendulum, or, the pendulum swinging. The dialectic appears almost as a back and forth phenomenon: first, this side, then to that side, first one, then two, then one again. It is not even clear that the process produces any advances. One cannot be certain that its motion can be construed as dialectic. Rather, it seems that the pathway simply moves back and forth, from one pole within contrariness to the other, back and forth, almost incessantly, and perhaps perpetually, back and forth, between one and two.

How should this be depicted except in terms which illustrate that contrariness is regulated by a certain binariness? Contrariness has been formed by a specific dialectic, a logic which applies uniquely to the interrelationship between terms that are conceived to be both sequential and contrary, simultaneously and recurrently. Even when the same polar terms come to function as principles of orientation, they mean very little, if anything, except in relation to one another. Thus to give emphasis to one of them is to imply something else about the other. To give emphasis to one of them is also to lend a certain strength to its counterpart. To lay stress on the term spirit, for example, means to take some exception to the term body. To develop a strategy for moving with change implies some definite attitude toward permanence or immobility. Permanence and change, therefore, are not only polar opposites; more specifically, they are also binary opposites.

In utilizing this language, we are drawing upon the contentions of the French anthropologist, Claude Lévi-Strauss, author of such prominent titles as *Tristes Tropiques, Structural Anthropology, The Elementary Structures of Kinship, The Savage Mind,* etc., and the chief architect of "the structuralist school" in anthropology, mythology, linguistics, literary theory, philosophy, sociology, and soon, it can be predicted, theology and religious studies as well. For it is to Lévi-Strauss's credit that he calls attention to the fundamental binary character of mental and social processes. He argues that human beings are disposed to formulate their apprehension of the world in terms of prominent contrasts: hot/cold, wet/dry, raw/cooked, nature/culture, animality/humanity, noise/silence, light/darkness, night/day, summer/winter, white/black, etc. Lévi-Strauss goes on to observe that these prominent sets of binary relations are implicit in the way in which we register and code information. The same binary relations underlie our language. They provide the terminology upon which we draw in defining our relation to the world.[5]

The prominent theological contrasts—body/spirit, time/eternity, freedom/authority, this world/the other world, etc., not to mention permanence/change—may be more than polar opposites. They may also be binary opposites. They come in pairs. Consequently, their respective careers stand and fall together. Each of the terms within these sets can be treated separately, but only through deliberate abstraction or artificial isolation. The terms belong together. They pertain together. They resonate together. They refer to each other, constantly, recurrently, perpetually, like alternating currents.

The methodology employed here has been designed to treat changes in religious consciousness by concentrating on the dialectical action that occurs within selected binary sets. There is much fluctuation within the binary sets, but the sets themselves appear to be constant within western religious consciousness. For this reason, ancient texts and classical religious figures continue to speak to "the modern situation." Meister Eckhart, St. John of the Cross, St. Bernard of Clairvaux, St. Francis of Assisi, St. Clare of Assisi, St. Theresa of Avila—the great company of mystics, saints, and martyrs—continue to be listened to. They can be listened to as though they were still present. Each of them reflects a quality of spiritual experience, an intensity of discipline, and a depth of religious insight that refuse to be qualified by the many centuries that separate them from our own era. None of their wisdom has been made obsolete by virtue of their relative place in history. As Jacob Needleman has emphasized, the question is not whether the great religious teachers can continue to teach, but whether the rest of us can bring ourselves to the place where we can learn. Learning has become problematical because it requires that "the parts of our inner nature are to come together if only for an instant." The real distance between teacher and learner is created by something other than history. The great religious personages retain the ability to teach, some say, more forcefully than ever. Their concerns—about the relation of body and spirit, about priorities between the realities of change and permanence, about the interdependence of freedom and authority—are identical to contemporary concerns. Indeed, in many instances the shared concern is expressed in identical form, sometimes even in the same language. The great company of mystics, saints, and martyrs could join the current dialogue and not feel out of step, phase, or context. For the insights of all sensitive religious persons within the western world have been formed by the same dialectical pendulum swings within the same contexts of reference. Morphologically, such insights have been binarial through and through.

While making methodological acknowledgments and confessions, we must say too that there is something of Anders Nygren's motif-research in our study.[6] Nygren described his work as comparative motif-research; our version of motif-research is more binarial than comparative, but motif-research it certainly is. When originally conceived, Nygren's technique was designed to help identify the Christian religion's dominant structural element. Our strategy has a similar intention. Following his analyses, Nygren reported that *agape* was the fundamental motif for Christianity, just as *nomos* performed the same function in Judaism and *eros* within Platonic religion. We have been content to identify *formal* structural factors, and have not extended our analysis to include descriptions of the content of the Christian religion. Nygren used motif-research to locate and describe large structural and systematic differences between religious orientations that grew up side by side. We have stayed within one unified, comprehensive structural system, and have not engaged in comparative analyses of selected religious traditions. Originally, motif-research was an extension of Nygren's more fundamental interest in locating religion's basic *apriori*.

Despite the differences in our approaches, there is much to be learned from Nygren's example of motif-tracing. Though it contained questionable identifications and interpretations, Nygren's was a pioneering effort in penetrating the dynamism of a constellation of religious affirmations by focussing on a central and formative thematic component. Nygren referred to this component as "that without which the constellation would not be what it is." As we have indicated, what makes a motif fundamental is that it performs this central and crucial *sine qua non* function. After identifying the fundamental motif, Nygren could attest, for example, that without *agape* Christianity would not be what it is. Turned the other way, because of *agape* Christianity is certainly what it most uniquely and characteristically is. Were the *agape* component missing, Christianity would simply not be what history has shown it to be. *Agape* is Christianity's most fundamental formative element. Christianity possesses other motifs of more or less central importance, but none have the crucial formative capacity of *agape*. The *agape* motif is that which most distinguishes Christianity from other religions. In Nygren's view, there simply is no other component whose function is as basic and formative.

This study has invested in motif-research too, for, like Nygren we have proceeded by identifying themes. Furthermore, like Nygren, we have worked with themes which possess formative structural capacities. That is, the themes we have dealt with are neither simply of incidental interest, nor are they of only relative value. But, unlike Nygren— this is the crucial point—*we have identified compound themes rather than simple ones*. It wouldn't do to isolate prominent themes simply on the basis that they have received considerable play within contemporary religious consciousness. There are such themes, of course, themes like hope, secularity, liberation, and the like. But none of these—as important and as prominent as they are—possess appropriate formative strength. About none of them can one say that its absence would make contemporary western religious consciousness something fundamentally different from what it is. This is not because any of the motifs are deficient. On the contrary, no matter how prominent such single themes might be, they still cannot qualify. They are of the wrong sort. Nygren's motifs are simple motifs; but Christianity's actual formative motifs are compound. They are compound, and they are binary. They always come in pairs. They always disclose themselves in contraries. They always possess built-in antipathies and antagonisms, and yet neither can completely discount the other without bringing distortion and destruction upon itself. For this reason our attempt to chart changes and transitions in contemporary western religious consciousness has focussed on the action that occurs *back and forth* between polar components of primary religious binary sets.

Nygren's genius was to recognize that certain elements give definitive structure to certain patterns of thought. It was understandable, then, that he would employ this insight to isolate and identify such elements. It is understandable, too, that he would try to reduce such elements to a single, primary, fundamental motif. He was looking for the one motif. His mistake was to presume that he could locate a single motif, and that it would be simple. In point of conceptual fact, the formative motif is always complex, and it seems to function in accordance with the logic of binariness. In motif-analysis, it is not enough to identify a simple element. The one must always be stipulated in relation to the two. One cannot talk about spirit, for example, without invoking talk about body. One cannot express the fundamentals of liberty without also describing bondage. One cannot attribute range to the world of change without saying something, if only by contrast, about the range of permanence. Without change one wouldn't know permanence. Unless there is body, it is not possible to define spirit. Freedom and bondage, too, are related to each other in this binarial way. To hold one is also to invoke the other. As we have indicated—as in the case of hot/cold, wet/dry, summer/winter, and the other clear binarial sets—two polar terms are always joined together. Indeed, it is the specific relationship between poles within a set which is most basically formative. In other words, it is the way in which contrariness is enunciated that gives a particular pattern of thought—or, more specifically, a given religious orientation—its distinctive shape and identifying characteristics.

But the intention of this book is not to concentrate on scholars' methodology. Important as that may be—especially to readers who have been professionalized into theology or religious studies—the real point concerns contrariness. If the argument of the book holds, contrariness can be expected to play a prominent role in religious affairs because of the way in which religious orientations are formed. Our analysis discloses that binary relationships are intrinsic to religious orientations. Because of this, one can expect a perpetual oscillation between binarial poles. We have cited several examples of binarial oscillation. We have also pointed to the drama: during the past decade religion's sensitivity has been affected by a series of reversals of prominent binarial arrangements. Several parallel binarial priorities were reversed abruptly, all at once.

Where does this leave the situation? Given the pervasive fact of contrariness, is the individual left simply to be a victim of the perpetual counterplay back and forth? Is there any control over the chain of realignments? Does the succession simply occur at will? Is religious sensitivity bound by the ongoing movement back and forth? Is there no place for free will, decision, creativity, and design? Must it be body orientation this year, then a return to body-subordinating spirituality next year? Does advocacy of change always lead to belated regard for permanence? Must permanence be modified by process? Is devotion to liberty retained, even to the point of personal frenzy, to be followed by recourse to a form of authority that promises some quiet? Will responsible involvement in social matrixes inevitably elicit a need for disengagement? Will the counterplay motion back and forth go on forever, without ending, unceasingly, incessantly, and persistently? Or is attachment to one mode or the other simply a matter of individual temperament? Does binary preference disclose primarily what sort of person one is? If so, can one be something or someone else? Does binary alternation indicate that one has become something or someone else? Can one be born anew? And, where binariness rules, can anything be done to break the bonds of contrariness? Are we back to Martin Luther's posing of the religious question: "What is the one thing absolutely necessary?"[7] Is there one thing absolutely necessary? When two choices are available, must one of them be denied so that religious sensitivity can find singularity? Has singularity a chance in a binarial world?

These are important questions, and religious experience during the past decade can be interpreted as an attempt to restore them. Indeed, individual and corporate experience during the past decade has brought the force of these questions to new religious consciousness. For, in talking about the dynamics of contrariness, we are also talking about the challenge of the counterculture. The counterculture was born in contrariness. Thus, in referring to the counterculture, we are identifying a specific constellation of religious, social, and cultural attitudes which contrariness formed. The meaning of counterculture, at least in part, is that a contrary principle—a contrary orientational element—was both resourceful and creative enough to produce a comprehensive and integrated world view. It was a counterview and a counterculture because it played upon the less dominant, less traditional, and anti-establishment side of contrariness.

To provide some perspective on the situation, let us back up a step to chronicle some of the events which led to the birth of the counterculture. We can be assisted in this venture by the impressive interpretative essay by Frank Kermode in a series of scholars' essays on changing conceptions of the humanities.[8] In his brief remarks, which are directed toward tracing the revolution in recent and contemporary consciousness, Kermode goes back to post World War I America to concentrate on the expressed expectations of people in the early 1930s. For the most part those large expectations met frustration and disappointment. Before long they were supplanted by a state of affairs that had not been anticipated. Kermode wonders why. And in retelling the story, Kermode draws upon a word which Ernst Bloch has inserted impressively into current conversation, the word *novum*. Kermode's analysis can be understood as a chronicle, or a sketch, of the fate of the *novum* in the contemporary era, a chronicle which finds the *novum* fated to failure.

Kermode states that in the 1930s "there was simply nowhere to go except into a new kind of world."[9] One of the indications of the power of this emerging *novum* is the early poetry of W. H. Auden, poetry which Kermode characterizes as being "strong and authoritative in its diagnosis of our hopeless ills, powerful though vague in its characterization of what was rushing at us 'out of the future into actual history.' "[10]   Something large was coming, and the prophecy seemed to foretell that the new revolution would be something more than a political revolution; it would entail the transformation of consciousness.

Something went wrong.   There was no revolution on behalf of a powerful, self-sustaining *novum*.   Instead there was disillusionment, then reversion and retrogression.   The debilitating events of the 1930s and 1940s are well known. Economic structures fell.   There was World War II. Dreams faded.   Hopes were postponed.   Then there was Franco and Stalin.   With all of this came a rigidification of an earlier—hitherto obsolete—corporate consciousness.   This is the telling event, for, in Kermode's view, it indicates that the earlier optimism was based on misconceptions of history.   The sense of history had not been perceived very well.   The optimism of the early 1930s wasn't sufficiently aware of the dynamics of cultural change. It was blatantly naive.   Kermode writes:

But our predictions and solutions were too simple. . . . Consequently, when the war ended, we retreated into [various] forms of worshiping pain and denying the natural man.   And only when that mood passed, and we began to assess the conduct and aspirations of the very young could we see, dimly enough, how it was that we were wrong, and why our arts and humanities had failed us.   Above all, we had made a bad mistake about something we pride ourselves on cherishing, namely, history.[11]

Consciousness had not been transformed.   It had taken some steps toward self-liberation, but these had been thwarted.   External events played influential, destructive roles.   But the larger issue pertains to degrees of cultural, ideological, and religious resilience. The new disposition incorporated some significant misreadings. Consequently, it was insufficiently resilient to live by the strength of its most innovative convictions.

Kermode's historical and cultural analysis is sharper and more specific. The naiveté of the early 1930s was due to a feeling of success regarding a previous attempt to reject the post-Renaissance world view. Kermode cites example after example from the works of poets, essayists, and artists prior to 1914 of this expressed feeling of success. Such pre-World War I optimism was carried forward even into the early 1930s. There were signs that the dreaded "post-Renaissance world" of "reason, intellect, and positivism" had yielded to a steady and persistent contrary upheaval. The post-Renaissance world had been a world of dissociation. But this world was being challenged by a new attempt to gain back association and interconnectedness. It was a movement on behalf of unity and integration. The "rancorous hatred of reason and intellect" had been countered by a-scientific, astrological, magical, and theosophical alternatives.

The idea that we live "in disconnection, dead and spiritless," because we have lost a unity of being that flowered and decayed at the Renaissance is still commonplace, and many important movements in the arts up to the Twenties can hardly be understood without some reference to this "dissociation."[12]

The irony is that the world that was acquired through the upheaval and transplantation process looked very much like the world that had been rejected. After the established world had been overthrown, its alternative looked very much like the established world. Kermode observes that the "new world" was built on a model which included a large and impressively atavistic requirement of order.

Something had been overlooked, or forgotten, in the process of metamorphosis. As a result, the finished product was not as radical as it could, or should have been:

We had forgotten a modernism which ridiculed "order," rejected the models which included it, and helped to invent the world we are going, for some time hence, to have to live in.[13]

Dada, an art form that flourished briefly early in the century, is Kermode's example of what might have been. Dada was violent and innovative beyond the proportions of anything the actual revolution produced. It was anti-post-Renaissance in a dramatic, profound, and self-conscious way. Its concept of order was thoroughly and "desacralizingly" modern. And yet, perhaps, the power of its suggestiveness was too great, or perhaps too confusing and debilitating. Dada was a more powerful movement than "the revolution" could sanction.

. . . it didn't on the whole seem effective, partly because of its palpable excesses and apparent unseriousness. In the Twenties, Dadaists became Surrealists and were otherwise assimilated into a more intelligible tradition.[14]

Dada implied a revolution that was not easily contained, but which, for sanity's sake, had to be contained. And yet, in the longer run, it proved to be both creative and productive:

But they [the Dadaists] invented the Happening, randomness as a policy, found art, and much else. And they changed not only our relation to the norms of the art of the past, but our relation to norms of conduct. For in the long run these things are related, though it proved a surprisingly long run, partly, because for a long time our attention was focused elsewhere.[15]

In referring to Kermode's example of the fate of Dada in the twentieth century, our purpose is not to debate the strengths and failures of this particular mode of art (or anti-art). Rather, it is to Kermode's principle of interpretation that we have been attracted. For Kermode suggests that in the twentieth century, the first really dramatic way of invoking a revolution in the arts and the humanities—and, eventually, in established modes of personal and social conduct—was rejected by those who, nevertheless, were advocating widespread cultural revolt and revolution. In their opting for a milder form of change, to their own eventual peril, these "revolutionaries" overlooked the insights and forgot the tenets of the more radical revolutionary movement. And in their own misreading of the dynamics of cultural change, they were shocked to find that the radical movement they had shunted aside had come back to haunt them in a manner they had not become equipped to tolerate. This sequence of movement, back and forth, according to Kermode, is responsible for the new revolution, that is, the counterculture revolution that gained full flowering in the 1960s. The counterculture enunciated some of the themes that had been offered to revolution by the Dadaists. It was the product of an oscillation. Sensing the irony in this situation, Kermode concludes:

In short, it is the modernism we neglected, and not the one we cultivated, that has, after lying dormant for half a century, erupted as the revolution of the counterculture.[16]

Robert N. Bellah, explains the intentions of the counterculture in a somewhat similar way.[17] For him, too, counterculture advocates have recourse to an attitude that had become lost, or lay hidden, from an earlier period in western man's corporate history. Like Kermode, Bellah also seizes upon a particular form of contrariness. But unlike Kermode, Bellah does not root the contrariness within successions of competing movements of thought. Rather his reference is to the conflict between subject and object that rages within the relationship between the self and the world. As Bellah views it, a prime goal of the counterculture was to forge a way beyond the subject-object split toward a meaningful form of wholeness or integration. In his recent Irving F. Laucks Lectures entitled "The Roots of Religious Consciousness," Bellah portrays counterculture advocates as expressing "something about reality and about the self, something about the whole which unites them, which did not make a clear distinction between subject and object." It is for this reason that counterculture advocates found themselves attractive to so-called primitive religion. Primitive religion becomes intriguing for it holds access to something primordial. It gives one the materials—and sometimes the method—by which to penetrate back to a time (or anti-time) of integration and wholeness. Its locus is prior to the birth of the contraries. Bellah describes the attractiveness of primitive religions:

. . . for two hundred years our culture has provided no other answer to any of our problems but more of the same. Under the circumstances, perhaps it is worth considering whether we might not have something to learn from those "ignorant," "backward," pre-modern societies that we have until yesterday despised. Perhaps they can tell us something about what to want, what we have forgotten in our mad dash for ever greater wealth and power.[18]

But it is not only primordial religious sensitivity that holds the prospect of a pre-binarial wholeness. There is also music. Bellah makes much of the music of the counterculture. It is unique, instructive, and deliberate in its intention to stimulate and support wholeness and integration.

Music is precisely a symbolic form of that kind, non-objective, uniting inner and outer, and it played an overwhelming central role in the history of the counterculture. Indeed the history of the counterculture is the history of its music. Another distinction central to the dominant scientific culture that the music of the counterculture broke through is the distinction between mental and physical, thought and action. Music can of course be a purely mental experience if the perceiving body remains passive. But it was just the point of countercultural musical expression that it involved general participation. A premium was put on producing rather than merely consuming music, and every young man and woman for a while seemed to be lugging around a guitar. And even when the music . . . was commercially produced in a concerto through records, the participation of the audience was supposed to be bodily. Through dancing, foot tapping or hand clapping, one was to become one with the music so that the distinction of inner and outer no longer made any sense. And such participation was seen as in primitive ritual to be restorative, life and energy giving.[19]

Music, drugs, the attempt to recover primitive or primordial religion—all of these, in Bellah's views, were designed to assist the recovery of a fundamental human integration and wholeness. All of them were instrumental to the revolt against contrariness.

Kermode's and Bellah's observations are instructive. Not only does each provide an intriguing account of the origin of counterculture, but each illustrates the exceedingly complex and delicate manner in which reflective self-consciousness is formed. Kermode's chronicle testifies that a particular style of expression, or pattern of cultural coherence, can burst forth fresh; then, because its implications are either too rich or novel to be tolerated, the same can lay dormant for awhile until it is reselected under different social, religious, and cultural circumstances. Portions of the counterculture belong to Dada-ism, Kermode suggests, though in altered guise. (Parenthetically, we can add that this is precisely the way in which Jürgen Moltmann accounts for the origin of the theology of hope: the perspective really belongs to the first century of Christian history, but, because its fundamental consequences were overwhelming, loss-of-nerve forced it underground until, biding its time, it was reselected, or rediscovered, rather recently, and, significantly, under counter-establishment-Christian auspices.)[20] Bellah provides an example of the same multi-faceted phenomenon in showing how the content of reflective self-consciousness is composed by the selection of materials from a past age, an era far removed from the contemporary frame of reference. In Kermode's example, a style of art and culture that had appeared earlier, briefly, at the beginning of the twentieth century, subsequently reappeared, largely imperceptibly and quite shockingly, when its cultural prerequisites had been established more pervasively. In Bellah's example, a style of art, religion, and culture, which many had regarded as being thoroughly outdated and obsolete—that is, downright primitive and archaic—was reselected and dressed up because of a newfound timeliness and propriety.

Both chroniclers offer their examples as clues to the meaning of counterculture. And both suggest that the path of reflective self-consciousness moves by these rhythms. The movement is never in a fixed direction, nor does it honor the regular sequential progression of time tenses. Past, present, and future become interchangeable. The past can be brought into the present as the present is viewed against the past. Using Ernst Bloch's phrase, there is indeed a "pull of the future," but that pull is often effected by a newfound attractiveness toward things past. Through the same conceptual mechanics, the present itself can become obsolete, that is, an antecedent to either the past or the future. Movement forward—wherever forward is—is never straight-line. Neither is it unalterable and irreversible. Instead the path of reflective self-consciousness is motivated creatively, innovatively, surprisingly, and sometimes shockingly, back and forth, in and out, up and down, always in accordance with the inklings, dictates, and urgings of new situations. To each new situation numerous responses are possible. Indeed, each generation selectively reshapes the past, redefines the present, and reenvisions the future in highly idiomatic and ideo-adaptive ways.

To be sure, many chroniclers of reflective self-consciousness have conceded that the future is open, more or less, and is thus given content by a constructive and creative selection process. But Kermode's and Bellah's examples seem to indicate that the past is open too. Indeed, where styles of thought and consciousness are concerned, there is no fixed past, but only a past that is formed out of the intricacies of the same selective process by which the present and the future are shaped.

An eloquent theoretical spokesmen on this subject is Stephen Toulmin, historian of science and author of the recent series, *Human Understanding*, the first volume of which is subtitled *The Collective Use and Evolution of Concepts*.[21] In this book, Toulmin attests that "men demonstrate their rationality not by ordering their concepts and beliefs in tidy formal structures, but by their preparedness to respond to novel situations with open minds." Though Toulmin's contentions were not calculated to apply specifically, if at all, to changes in religious conceptions, they lend much insight to the issues with which we are dealing. In criticizing Thomas Kuhn's and others' work on the function of paradigms and models in the organization of thought, Toulmin provides the following description of the new task in conceptual chronicling:

What we need . . . is an account of conceptual development which can accommodate changes of any profundity, but which explains gradual and drastic change alike as alternative outcomes of the same factors working together in different ways.[22]

Certainly the changes we are examining in this study belong to the same conceptual genre as those for which Toulmin wants to provide an account. As we have seen, changes in contemporary religious consciousness, "gradual and drastic" alike, can be depicted as "alternative outcomes of the same factors working together in different ways." And we can draw upon Kermode's and Bellah's analyses as analogous cases in point. Kermode provided an example of clear binarial alternation, where the gist of the large current binarial reversal had been prefigured, though fleetingly, in an earlier breakthrough event. Bellah focussed on an attempt to recapture a pre-binarial wholeness, that is, an attempt to be set free from the clutches, or the perpetual oscillation, of binarial opposition. But in both illustrations, binarial opposition and/or binarial alternation was at work.

From all of these accounts, it appears that shifts in reflective self-consciousness—whether factored as religious self-consciousness or not—do not occur according to straight-line-forward movement, in predictable ways, in accordance with a fixed destination. Rather, the situations we have confronted have been remarkably flexible, malleable, and amenable to novelty. To state this is not to conclude that there is no logic to religious change, however. On the contrary, using Toulmin's language, religious change is an outcome of "the same factors working together in different ways." We have suggested that binarial alternation provides a clue to the dynamics of religious transformation. Thus, as the persistent agent of transformation, binarial alternation also insures that the same factors are sustained, in different patterns of formulation.

In other words, Hegel is too pompous; and, process-wise, Anders Nygren's scheme is naive. The true picture of change belongs to a model in which the constants are not ascribed to permanence—and thus really reside outside change—but are identified as the formal factors, or the structural factors, without which neither could be nor be discerned.

But we are ready now to step back into this book's major sequence of development. When we left the chronicle, we had discussed several prominent instances of binary alternation in contemporary religious consciousness. After introducing some parallel cases, we concentrated on the fate of a major contemporary theological orientation, the theology of hope, and we had considered some of the implications of a growing religious mood, herein referred to as "positive disengagement." It is time for us now to return to the chronicle, to weave some of these larger strands together.

NOTES

1. Frank Kermode, "Revolution: The Role of the Elders," in *Liberations. New Essays on the Humanities in Revolution,* ed. Ihab Hassan (Middletown: Wesleyan University Press, 1971), p. 97.

2. August Comte, *Cours de philosophie positive,* as available in *The Positive Philosophy of August Comte,* introd. Abraham E. Blumberg (New York: AMS Press, 1974).

3. Raimundo Panikkar's development of this theme was presented in a paper during the University of California symposium in honor of Mircea Eliade, Santa Barbara, California, November 14–16, 1974. The proceedings of the symposium are being prepared for publication through the Institute of Religious Studies, University of California, Santa Barbara.

4. See, for example, Paul Ricoeur, "The Symbol—Food for Thought," *Philosophy Today* 4 (1960): 196–207.

5. Claude Lévi-Strauss, *The Elementary Structures of Kinship,* trans. James Harle Bell, John Richard von Sturmer, ed. Rodney Needham (Boston: Beacon Press, 1969); *The Raw and the Cooked,* trans. John and Doreen Weightman (New York: Harper Torchbooks, 1969); *The Savage Mind* (Chicago: University of Chicago Press, 1969); *Structural Anthropology,* trans. Claire Jacobson and Brooke Grundfest Schoepf (Garden City: Doubleday and Company, 1967); *The Scope of Anthropology,* trans. Sherry Ortner and Robert A. Paul (London: Jonathan Cape, 1967); *Totemism,* trans. Rodney Needham (Boston: Beacon Press, 1963); *Tristes Tropiques,* trans. John Russell (New York: Atheneum, 1972). See also the studies of Lévi-Strauss by Edmund Leach, *Claude Lévi-Strauss* (New York: Viking Press, 1970); *Structuralism,* ed. Jacques Ehrmann (Garden City: Doubleday and Company, 1970); *Introduction to Structuralism,* ed. Michael Lane (New York: Basic Books, 1970); and *Claude Lévi-Strauss. The Anthropologist as Hero,* ed. E. Nelson Hayes and Tanya Hayes (Cambridge: The Massachusetts Institute of Technology Press, 1970).

6. I refer specifically to Anders Nygren's works, chiefly, *Agape and Eros,* trans. Philip S. Watson (London: S.P.C.K., 1938); *Religiöst Apriori* (Lund, 1921); *Filosofi och motivforskning* (Stockholm, 1940); and *Meaning and Method,* trans. Philip S. Watson (Philadelphia: Fortress Press, 1972).

7. Martin Luther, "The Freedom of a Christian," in *Luther's Works,* eds. Jaroslav Pelikan and Helmut T. Lehmann (Philadelphia: Fortress Press, 1957), Vol. 31, pp. 327–377. The original text is Luther's *Tractatus de Libertate Christiani,* in *D. Martin Luthers Werke* (Weimar: Kritische Gesamtausgabe, 1883), Vol. VII.

8. Frank Kermode, "Revolution: The Role of the Elders," *Liberations,* pp. 87–99.

9. Ibid., p. 89.

10. Ibid.

11. Ibid., p. 90.

12. Ibid.

13. Ibid., pp. 91–92.

14. Ibid., p. 92.

15. Ibid.

16. Ibid., p. 94.

17. Robert N. Bellah, "The Roots of Religious Consciousness," given as the Irving F. Laucks Lectures on the Science of Man, sponsored by the Institute of Religious Studies, University of California, Santa Barbara, April 1974.

18. Ibid.

19. Ibid.

20. See Moltmann's chronicle in his essay, "What is 'New' in Christianity: The Category *Novum* in Christian Theology," in *Religion, Revolution, and the Future,* trans. M. Douglas Meeks (New York: Charles Scribner's Sons, 1969).

21. Stephen Toulmin, *Human Understanding,* Vol. I, *The Collective Use and Evolution of Concepts* (Princeton: Princeton University Press, 1972).

22. Ibid., p. 122.

PART THREE

PROJECTIONS

CHAPTER SIX

THE RETURN OF
HOMO EREMETICUS

"Catholicism believes in both an interior God and an exterior God.   Such is the religious formula for its contradictions."

—Maurice Merleau-Ponty[1]

Contrary currents in contemporary religious consciousness rested prominently on my mind one misty, foggy, wistful Sunday morning as Lois, the children, and I wended our way up a narrow, winding, switch-backed, partially asphalt road in the Santa Lucia mountains, one mile south of Lucia, and a few miles south of Big Sur, California.   Our destination: the Immaculate Heart Hermitage.   Our intention: to worship with the Camaldolese hermits at their Sunday morning mass.   We had vacationed in the area before, and had been intrigued by the simple white cross that stands alongside Highway 1, Cabrillo Highway, at the entrance to the mountain road leading to the Hermitage.   We had been partially prepared by one of the hermits who later became a friend of ours in Santa Barbara, and by tales told by others who had journeyed to the hermitage, either as visitors or as retreatants.   We knew of the strict austerity of the hermits.   We knew something of the hours they keep, their daily schedule that calls for rising for the first liturgy and prayers of the day shortly after midnight, then, following sleep, before 6 a.m. for the service of lauds.   We couldn't forget what one of the hermits had said:

the privilege of breaking our sleep to rise in the middle of the night to praise God while others continue to sleep—this in our life has always been one of my greatest joys.[2]

We had known something of their diet—meatless, but generous, except on Fridays and during penitential seasons. We had even heard something about the recluses among the hermits, those who join the other hermits only a few times during the year. Perhaps for reasons of "positive disengagement," we were curious. But we are not alone. Because of its proximity to the Esalen Institute, which is a few miles north of Lucia, travelers—or pilgrims—frequently try to visit both locations, suspecting that each might be a contemporary example of sacred or consecrated space. Others were there that day. Others would continue to come. We took William Irwin Thompson's description of his journey to the hermitage with us; we relied upon his description of the road up the mountainside as a guidebook, to give us some indication of where we were, and how far we should have to travel.[3]

The hermitage itself appeared in gloriously mixed fog and sunshine. We parked the car in the visitors area, grateful that the so-called "dieseling" by which it is affected sometimes (when the motor continues to run, or chug, uncertainly, even after the ignition switch has been turned off) didn't interfere with the initiation process. One of the hermits, the guest master, came out to meet us. I told him quickly and briefly who we were. In response to several hurried questions, he assured me that children were permitted to attend mass too.

The celebrant and homilist this day was an older man, slightly bent and balding, with a distinctive English accent. The text on which he based his sermon was the epistle reading of the day, from the 12th chapter of the Letter to the Hebrews. He focussed on the verse "whom the Lord loves he chastens, and every son whom he receives he scourges," giving his exposition of the reading distinct eremetical twists. As he spoke, I thought of the self-consciousness which he himself had both to explore and to endure, a self-consciousness which must be heightened and made more intense by life in the hermit's cell. I wondered how he could bear it. I recalled Thomas Merton's writing that in the cell, in contemplation, when one is alone with himself, he is brought to "the heart-rending discovery that Auschwitz, Hiroshima, Vietnam and Watts are present in the intimate core of his own being."[4] I wondered to what extent discipline pertains to the ability to live with and tolerate one's own thoughts, and whether scourging is part of the intense and repeated self-facing which must occur there, in solitude, hour after hour. But I was jolted from such reflections by the analytical delight I find in trying to predict the outcome of sermons, almost unconsciously, even before I have heard them all the way through. My Lutheran instincts had taught me to suspect that the emphasis upon personal discipline would detract from the gospel's stressing of grace. But there was nothing to worry about, for the hermit-priest, bent, speaking deliberately and slowly, almost pleading, went on to note that the true saints of God know how fully they are dependent upon divine grace, while those who strive on their own behalf suffer assorted vulnerabilities, distortions, misalignments, and interior failures. Once again, I thought about intense self-consciousness, perhaps because there are aspects of it I have come to fear. Did he mean that even within the life of contemplation there is a movement beyond contemplation, an act or event by which the very mechanisms of interiority are either cancelled, negated, or bracketed? Did he mean that one experiences an inner release, from time to time, even from interiority itself? Is this what the monk experiences in mystical awareness? It must be, and yet all of this occurs interiorly. How, then, within the self is the transfer from self- to divine-dependence negotiated? How does grace effect release from solitude in the very posture of solitude? Doesn't this imply that the interior life is multidimensional, or multilayered? Then, are the dynamics of the *vita con-templativa* regulated by the same multilayeredness which is present in contemporary religious trends? Is the movement or passage from state to state that which St. Theresa of Avila sought to describe in her several tiered *Interior Castle?*[5] Are these the same as the rhythms Søren Kierkegaard chronicled?[6] And what is there where this interior action occurs? Was the hermit-priest, bent, deliberate, pleading, entreating, talking about himself as much as he was talking to the rest of us, hermits and non-hermits alike? And in talking about himself, was he, by definition, talking about the rest of us? Certainly this form of solitariness is much to be prized over the constant being-with-others that often only enhances isolation. It is of a different grade than the loneliness one can feel in the midst of anti-solitude.

We stayed for awhile, even after the mass had ended. There was a woman there, a wife and mother whose husband and children had come with her to the mass. Like us, she was a visitor to the hermitage that day. Boldly, using language that revealed a lack of Sunday influence, she asked one of the hermits, "which version of the Bible do you use here?" The reply, "Oh, we use many different translations." The initial question was followed with another, "but which translation was used in this morning's service?" The hermit responded by moving to the book shelf, reaching up for a paperback version of the New

Testament portion of *The New Jerusalem Bible.* He handed her a copy. She went outside, thumbing through the pages of the same Bible the hermits read, that days' authorized version, as she walked along, slowly, on one of the pathways leading away from the chapel. Then she sat down on a bench. And as her husband, children, and some other persons—visitors too—sat or stood alongside of her, she began reading passages from the New Testament aloud. One passage after another she read aloud to herself and to them, as they remarked on the use of the English language, and asked rhetorical questions about the meaning of what they were hearing. As we drove away, they were still sitting and standing there, still in that mysterious blending of fog and sunshine, with the hermit-priest standing at some distance behind them, comprehending them, almost as if, whether they needed to be aware of it or not, he was blessing them.

Coming down the mountain later, little Laura, our younger daughter, said "Daddy, we're going the wrong way." Could she have known what Lois and I were sensing, that, after too long a time, we had come to discover spirituality? Was this the point "beyond the edge of history" as Thompson called it? Was there any other place to go after one had been to the top of this mountain? Would any way have been the wrong way? Wouldn't any destination have been a letdown, a comedown, after we had been to the mount of transfiguration? Wasn't this the way beyond contrariness? Wasn't Laura's urge, and ours, similar to Peter's in the transfiguration story in the New Testament: "Lord, let's build three tents [or tabernacles, or cells] here." Can't we stay here? Are we not allowed to tarry here, on this consecrated ground, where one's orientation to life seems supported by utter simplicity? Do we have to go the other ways, the usual ways, where one's place in life, no matter how profound and resolute, seems riddled with confliction? Why must singularity always be qualified by contrariness? If we could but stay, would our attitudes remain single? Or did contrariness exist even here?

Perhaps it was our brief sojourn on the mountain that dazzled us against seeing it. Perhaps, then, the sojourn ought to be as brief as possible so that tarrying isn't allowed to spoil the force of those integrating insights. But, then, is the way beyond contrariness only fleeting, lasting for only a moment, until, suddenly and abruptly, the pilgrim finds himself mired in confliction again? Can one abide in the locus of simplicity, where, truly, as Kierkegaard said, purity of heart is to will one thing? And what is the locus of this locus, right now? What is the there where being here now is now-here and nowhere, and here-where is every-where, all and nothing both at once, and once at both? Had we come to what, for us, was a temporary resting place, where, at least for awhile, contrariness had been stilled because its dialectic ceased to rule? Was this a place where polar opposition, at least for awhile, had been neutralized and temporized? Perhaps it will take some time before we know for sure. But we came away from the hermitage sensing something more of the force of the blending of contemplative and active religious temperaments, such as one finds in the figure of St. Francis of Assisi, Gandhi, Thomas Merton, and, as his autobiographical documents reveal, Nathan Söderblom, the late, great Archbishop of the Church of Sweden. I mention the latter with particular enthusiasm for he is not often numbered in the company of these other contemplative saints, and he deserves to be.[7]

It was a big day, a full day, indeed, a rare, complete day. But as we look back on it now, we can fit it to a larger perspective. Viewed sequentially, the monastery of Poor

Clares in Santa Barbara provided the occasion of first compelling exposure. The visit to New Camaldoli gave supporting evidence, intriguing extensions, and additional
content. But before the disposition had run its course there
were additional visits, stopovers, and brief stays at other
monasteries and centers of contemplative life throughout
the country, as well as hopes and plans for return visits to
monasteries we had known years before in Europe, where,
as a family, we traveled from place to place, in pilgrimage,
in a Volkswagen camper.

The largest single development occurred in conjunction
with another undergraduate class at the University of California, Santa Barbara, this one deliberately designed to
devote an academic quarter's attention to "the contemplative impulse in western culture." The rationale was easy
to state: the contemplative tradition, though not as well
known, belongs as much to the West as it does to the East;
without conscious recognition of its place, we fail to grasp
one of the primary components of our cultural heritage.
From there one can proceed to argue that lack of attention
to the contemplative tradition leads to an impoverished
sense of our own resources and capacities. And from there
one can suggest that the revival of interest in spirituality in
our time is a direct result of the intense over-preoccupation
with materialistic values and pragmatic sanctions. For
whatever reasons, enrollment in the class was large. Enthusiasms ran high throughout the academic quarter as students
and instructor alike recognized that a deep reservoir was
being tapped, and perhaps also that a significant contemporary religious trend had been identified.

As part of their work in the course, students were encouraged to visit monastic centers in the surrounding area.
Almost all of them did this on at least one occasion, and

several more than once. This was the "field-work" component of the class, and it was understood to be ancillary to the required reading for the course, the research in the library on classical forms of monasticism, the role of contemplation in the West, etc. It turned out to be a particularly good assignment for the male students, though considerably more difficult for the women because of rules of cloister. But some of the monasteries were open to men and women, and there were convents available primarily to women. Because of the field-work component, the class itself became a forum or home-station to which the temporary or weekend pilgrim would return after visiting a monastery, or speaking with a contemplative, to tell of his or her adventures.

Many of the students kept track of their thoughts while experiencing the life of the monastery, jotting them down in diaries or journals. The temper of their experience is reflected in the journal jottings of a male student during his visit to New Camaldoli:

R. and I arrived at the Immaculate Heart Hermitage seven hours ago and have already begun to speak in the hushed tones of monastic silence. My naive eagerness to experience the religious life has been dampened by the humanness of the monks. I am realizing that one does not leave humanity behind in accepting the monastic life, but finds all of its complexities within the walls of the silent enclosure. The men here (at least the two I've spoken with) have greeted me with intense interest and warm acceptance. It is this penetrating personal attentiveness coupled with what I can only describe as *active silence* that immediately touches me. They have begun to unconsciously live the silent life; hermits in the world. It is as if their minds are at another level, always responding to you with a certain excited preoccupation.

The next morning he wrote the following:

I woke up this morning to a beautifully clear horizon. As I looked out over the deep blue Pacific Ocean 1300 feet below I was struck by the mystical *endlessness* of this world. The clouds forming a misty cotton-white line between the dark blue sea and the light blue sky seem to suggest a continuity of reality where only the mind can follow. It is as if I'm looking at the end of the world—a world of reality beyond which is another world. How does one describe a "beyond" except in terms of its edge?

Then, regarding his attempt to adjust to the daily schedule or regime of the monks:

I'm finding it difficult to adjust my hours to the hours of the life here. As a late night person, I seem to be going to sleep just as Vigils begin. Naturally, I then sleep through Lauds (I was awake but had gotten the *time* wrong, 6:15 instead of 6:45). One can adjust to this schedule, I'm sure; whether I can is a question of motivation. It is clear, however, that a great deal of self-discipline is necessary to live this life. It is not "all things in moderation" but rather "God in adoration" in all that the monks do.

A subsequent journal entry from the same day:

Already I realize that the many questions which I brought here, about vocation, relationships, hopes and dreams, will not be answered in the time I have available. Perhaps what will occur is a settling of my frantic pace of worry. I see the temptation to use my time only resting and not creatively thinking. The settling-in I speak of is a type of integration of self—in my case a religious self that allows diversity and creativity within a boundary of faith. This has been a problem for me from the beginning—how to be free to be faithful. Worship (or the lack of it) has been my focus, a touchstone of religious expression. Sometimes deeply fulfilling, sometimes shallow and irritating, I have always felt drawn to it.

This morning I offer my prayers to the hidden altar of God, beyond the distant changing horizon.

Then, following additional detailed references to situations at home on which he was reflecting, references of a more individually personal nature, the student completed his account with this record of his state of mind before leaving the hermitage:

I'm prepared to leave—at least everything is ready except me. I must go and yet don't want to. How can I express the depth I've been able to see and hear while I've been here? Perhaps it is the life; perhaps the men it attracts; perhaps both and some X factor that gives substance to the time and form to the silence. I know that I cannot penetrate this secret even one inch if I try but that a grace to experience it must be given. Paradoxically, one can only receive this gift if one is in the *right time* and has listened to the words in the silences. Truly God meets man in unexpected places and unexpected ways.

Brother A's last words for us students: "Be aware of the poverty and the riches and how one gets them." Divesting one's self in order to reach God is no easier for a monk than for anyone else. For us the misleading richness of knowledge may be a barrier to this true richness with God. Be simple and poor.

Goodbye to all that I see and hear. May you share your richness with others yet to arrive.

The cloud bank is moving inland and soon I will be unable to see the ocean—Yet I will still know that the ocean is there. Perhaps this is what I take with me, that I still know God's presence outside the personal confines of monastic life. If this is the case I have received a rich gift, and at least part of my quest has begun.

Many of the reports brought back to the class were of the same tone, overwhelmingly positive, giving repeated evidence of having been touched or moved by encounters with silence. Significantly, the students seemed to prefer the monastic centers which exhibited the most austere forms of religious life. It was evident that they had enrolled in the course for a variety of personal reasons, and that in their choice of term projects they had taken the opportunity to pursue something out of the ordinary.

There were numerous guides along the way, pilgrims who had frequented some of the same places earlier and had left diary or journal accounts for the rest of us to read. For example, after reading his *At the Edge of History* and *Passages about Earth*, one can understand why William Irwin Thompson would be engaged in an effort to establish a monastery (though not on an exclusively Christian religious base), appropriately called Lindisfarne (denoting deliberate, strategic Celtic religious ties) in Southampton, on the furthermost point on New York's Long Island.[8] After reading his *The New Religions* as well as *Religion for a New Generation*, one can also perceive something of Jacob Needleman's intention in making a summer's pilgrimage through Europe, going from monastery to monastery, all the way to the famous spiritual centers on Mt. Athos in the mountains of Greece, asking pointed questions about the relation of "sacred tradition" to "present religious need."[9]

Certainly Thompson and Needleman are not alone. The enthusiasm with which the summer academic program in western spirituality at Western Michigan University in Kalamazoo has been received points to the currency as well as the resiliance of the new monastic interest. Significantly, the Western Michigan University program is being cosponsored by the Mediaeval Studies Institute and the Center for Spiritual Studies, supported by a grant from the National Endowment for the Humanities which was arranged for, in part, by a monastic order.

But the truly significant intellectual development occurred through an encounter with the writings and teachings of Thomas Merton, the late Trappist monk who, prior to his death in 1968, had done so much to bring about monastic reform and to reawaken and rekindle contemplative sensibilities in the west. Merton was immediately attractive to many of the students because, unlike some authorized Christian spokesmen, he had firsthand knowledge of the religions of the Asian world as well as a keen appreciation for them. Furthermore, he found the religious insights of Asian monks so fascinating that he sought to learn about the dynamics of the spiritual life from them. For him, it was inappropriate to initiate a dialogue with representatives of Asian religions on doctrinal or even quasi-ideological grounds. Merton's fundamental interest lay not in doctrinal formulations—though he was a gifted thinker—but in inwardness, that is, spirituality or interiority. And, in this respect in particular, he was acutely aware that he had much in common with his Asian monastic counterparts. His openness was refreshing.

Merton was immediately attractive to students and instructors for another reason: he seemed to grasp what was intended via the counterculture. He had an innate sense of the significance of the attempt to offer a social, cultural, and political alternative to prevailing and established world structures. Of course, the link between monasticism and counterculture has a long history. As conceived by its founders, monasticism itself was a kind of counterculture because it offered an alternative to the established patterns of being in the world. The interest was more than lip service on Merton's part. He was taken by the writings of the Marxist philosopher, Herbert Marcuse, for example.[10] Indeed, he agreed with some Marxist students who told him that they were the true monks. It was not difficult for him to conceive of the monastic alternative in counterculture terms: "The monk belongs to the world, but the world belongs to him insofar as he has dedicated himself totally to liberation from it in order to liberate it."[11]

Thus, the teaching made prominent in Asian religions, that the world is illusion or deception, came naturally with Merton, although not unambiguously so. He had much to say about the artificiality of the status quo, for example, and, along with advocates of the counterculture, had sought a workable individual and corporate alternative.

When Merton engaged in comparative reflection on the world's religious traditions, his significant cues were taken from the works of R. C. Zaehner, the late Oxford University historian of religions whose formulations of the relation of Christian to non-Christian religions was influenced by the conceptual orientation of Teilhard de Chardin. Following Zaehner, Merton was disposed to approach non-Christian religions as something other than alternative or competing ideological systems. Zaehner recognized, and Merton seems to agree, that truth is never the product of patronage in religion. One may find expressions of the truth in a variety of textual loci, but this need not imply that all texts are somehow speaking the truth. Nor does it mean that everything said in any one religion is true. Religions may or may not be authentic, but Zaehner would have a difficult time speaking about "true religions." In Zaehner's view, religions are neither comprehensively true nor comprehensively false. Religions are neither true nor false, but sometimes express truths and sometimes express convictions which are short of the truth.[12]

Merton, of course, was partial to the Catholic faith. In it he lived, he breathed, and was faithfully nurtured. At the same time, his attitude to Catholicism was such that he was quite receptive to the religious insights of other traditions, and, in some specific areas, he had no hesitancy in admitting that the religious experience of others was and is more profound than that of Christians. Thus, his personal identification with the Catholic faith did not make him rigid or otherwise defensive in his attitude to non-Catholics, particularly to Buddhist teaching. On the contrary, he perceived large and expansive areas of shared insight. This was not inconsistent with his being a strongly committed Catholic. Nor did he feel obliged, as others in similar situations have, to baptize everything "Christian" or "Catholic" as the price of acceptance or sanctionability. His attitude belonged to the spirit of the stance toward non-Christian religions cultivated in scholarship by Zaehner, which, in Merton's case, provided a seriousness, openness, and accessibility to other traditions of individual and corporate spirituality.

But the attraction to Merton is stimulated not only by his openness to the insights of non-western and non-Christian religions. It is also encouraged by his adoption of a process view of reality, a view, which, by Merton's own confession, articulates very well with the attitude of Teilhard de Chardin, the French Jesuit evolutionist-paleontologist-theologian, as well as with Zaehner's perspective. Both Teilhard and Zaehner tended to view reality according to progressive, process categories. Merton was also very acutely conscious of the world scheme that process orientations had attempted to supplant, that is, the conception of the universe as a "cause and effect mechanism" which is regulated by a supreme being "outside" or "above" the world who stands to the world primarily as "First Cause" or "Prime Mover." According to this hierarchical, non-process view, deity is defined as follows:

He is the Uncaused Cause, guiding, planning, willing every effect down to the tiniest detail. He is regarded as a Supreme

Engineer. But men can enter into communication with Him, share in His plans, participate in His causation by faith and prayer. He delegates to men a secret and limited share in His activity in so far as they are united with him.[13]

A transformation is necessary for two major reasons. For one, the former religious conception of reality, which Merton refers to as "the classical way of viewing the world," cannot be reconciled with post-Newtonian physics. It lacks scientific credibility, and thus philosophical respectability. But, even more significantly, Merton charges the classical viewpoint as being "religiously uninspiring." This is a fundamental charge. It isn't enough that the traditional religious outlook lacks scientific sense. Beyond that, it isn't even positively religious. Indeed, it leaves persons of religious sensitivity nonplussed.

The alternative to the classical view is a dynamic conception of the relation of God and the world. Instead of being placed outside or above the world, God is depicted as being immanent in life processes. "God is at work in and through man, perfecting an ongoing creation."[14] This was Teilhard's vision. It became Merton's.

For Merton, however, the significance of this revised conception of the universe is directly related to the geographical setting in which Teilhard lived during the time he was formulating his views. Merton asks, "Where did Teilhard acquire this perspective?" Then he answers his own question: "In the deserts of Asia, in the vast solitudes which were in many ways more 'monastic' than the cloisters of our monastic institutions."[15] Teilhard's was the vision of one who dwelled in the desert, the wilderness, or the wasteland.

It is worth pausing on this point simply to recall that monastic experience, from its very inception in the West, has been integrally associated with the desert. For example, St. Anthony of Egypt, the first Christian monastic, lived his life in the desert, established monasticism as a form of Christian life both appropriate to and facilitated by the awareness of desert. The geographical correspondences between Teilhard, Anthony, and the others is a significant observation. But the deeper side of this concerns the way in which "the desert" functions and symbolizes the religious life. For desert has always been a symbol for emptiness, wilderness, exile, and alienation. Thus, it turns out that desert monastic experience and Marxist thought concentrate on a common theme, *alienation*. Both understand the human person to be an exile, an alien, in a world in which he is under control or subjection to a dominant, hostile force. Significantly, Merton suggests that it was Teilhard's recogni‑ tion of this factor, from within the desert context, that increased his sensitivity to a dynamic, immanentist, process orientation to human life. By virtue of the very context out of which he reflected on the meaning of the Christian life, Teilhard was indeed a monk.

The similarities between Moltmann and Merton can be made apparent in their mutual dependence upon and ad‑ miration for Dietrich Bonhoeffer. To be sure, Bonhoeffer plays a much larger role in Moltmann's than in Merton's formulations. In a variety of ways Moltmann's theology can be understood as an extension of Bonhoeffer's position. We have pursued this subject in earlier chapters. Bon‑ hoeffer does not play the same role for Merton. Indeed, there is but scant reference to Bonhoeffer. And yet the key reference is direct, illuminating, and relates to a crucial element in Merton's orientation.

After noting that Teilhard came to the Christian faith in terms of process, evolutionist pattern in direct association with his being in the desert, Merton speaks about Bonhoeffer and his life in the prison cell.

Bonhoeffer, regarded as an opponent of all that monasticism stands for, himself realized the need for certain "monastic" conditions in order to maintain a true perspective in and on the world. He developed these ideas when he was awaiting his execution in a Nazi prison.[16]

One can perceive much more in the passage than incidental reference to Bonhoeffer, or even intriguing temperamental inter-associations between Bonhoeffer and Teilhard. By playing upon the terms "deserts," "vast solitudes," "monastic conditions," "prison," etc., and making equivalences wherever these are appropriate, one can place both Teilhard and Bonhoeffer within an authentic and fundamental monastic context.

The symbol of medieval monasticism is the wall and the cloister. Instead of merely being self-enclosed, the modern monk might perhaps emulate Teilhard in the desert of Mongolia or Bonhoeffer in prison. These are more primitive and more authentic examples of what a charismatic solitude can mean.[17]

But there is more, for the passage also makes us aware that we are dealing with a genre of literature—Teilhard's, Bonhoeffer's, Merton's, and perhaps even Moltmann's perspectives belonging to it—which emphasizes the vantage points open to those in the cell. In a special way, Bonhoeffer was monastic too.

Human alienation was Merton's most pervasive and persistent theme. It was present in the beginning, in his autobiographical, *The Seven Storey Mountain,* and was the subject of his final address at the conference in Bangkok in 1968. The preoccupation with alienation articulates well with Merton's lifelong intrigue with Marxist philosophy.

The Marxist perspective fascinated Merton. But it was the Marxist diagnosis of present ills rather than prescriptions for resolution which he found compelling. He was taken by the Marxist analyses of current world problems, particularly its critique of *western capitalism.*

That criticism proposes, in short, that capitalism is a fundamental deterrent to the progress and eventual maturation of the human race. Merton addressed this subject under the theme of "the dehumanization of man," within which context he could also refer to the *hybris* of man in capitalist based technological society. In *Contemplation in a World of Action,* Merton wrote:

> We think of Marx as simply saying that capitalism must be overthrown, and as being "against private property," therefore against natural law, but one idea that he investigated in depth was the dehumanization of man in industrial society. His remedy was not just revolution, but that man must own the means of production which he uses; he must not be reduced to the level of an object or a machine to be used by someone else: he must preserve his dignity as a man.[18]

In the same essay, Merton addresses the predicament of man in technological society. The problem is that societies based on the capitalist structure do not enhance man's quest for maturity, but instead more firmly fix man in "infantilism and irresponsibility."

> . . . the elaborate conventional structures of thought, language, etc., are all doing the exact opposite from what they originally pretended to do: instead of bringing man in contact with reality, and helping him to be true to himself, they are standing between man and reality as veils and deceptions. They prevent him from facing "anguish."[19]

This is a consistent theme in Merton's writings. As early as *The Seven Storey Mountain,* for example, he wrote:

It is true that the materialistic, the so-called culture that has evolved under the tender mercies of capitalism, has produced what seems to be the ultimate limit of this worldliness. And nowhere, except perhaps in the analogous society of pagan Rome, has there ever been such a flowering of cheap and petty and disgusting lusts and vanities as in the world of capitalism, where there is no evil that is not fostered and encouraged for the sake of making money. We live in a society whose whole policy is to excite every nerve in the human body and keep it at the highest pitch of artificial tension, to strain every human desire to the limit and to create as many new desires and synthetic passions as possible, in order to cater to them with the products of our factories and printing presses and movie studios and all the rest.[20]

Then, in his final address, after commenting favorably on the theories of Marcuse, Merton speaks about the current (1968) disturbances and revolutions in the universities as lucid examples of the same phenomena:

Marcuse and the students who are revolting in the universities contend that . . . significant choices can no longer be made in the kind of organized society you have either under capitalism or under Soviet Russia. The choices that are really important have all been made before you get around to trying it yourself. The choices that are left to us are insignificant choices like the choice between which toothpaste I will use, which airline I will take . . . and so on.

The idea of alienation is basically Marxist, and what it means is that man living under certain economic conditions is no longer in possession of the fruits of his life. His life is not his. It is lived according to conditions determined by somebody else.[21]

All of it, of course, is background to his concept of *alienation*, a concept which is central to both Marxist and Christian thought. Within the Marxist context, alienation means that "one is not in possession of his life." In monastic language, alienation means that, as Merton puts it, "in one way or another . . . the claims of the world are fraudulent."[22]

The primary metaphor remains that of the pilgrim in the desert. The Christian's self-understanding is that of an alien or exile in a world in which he is not in control. But, significantly, Merton applies the metaphor both exteriorly and interiorly. Exteriorly, one lives as an exile because of social and political oppression, whether implicit or overt. Interiorly, there is alienation because the heart is a waste-land. There is inner emptiness, a duality within. The desert is both exterior and interior. In the Bangkok address, for example, Merton said:

Buddhist and Christian monasticism start from the problem inside man himself. Instead of dealing with the external structures of society, they start with man's own consciousness. Both Christianity and Buddhism agree that the root of man's problems is that his consciousness is all fouled up and he does not apprehend reality as it fully and really is; that the moment he looks at something, he begins to interpret it in ways that are prejudiced and predetermined to fit a certain wrong picture of the world.[23]

This wrong way of viewing the world has both exterior and interior sides, both of which stem from the propensity to place the individual ego in the center of things. This is an impossible stance. One cannot be in the center of things if the conditions for centering are not present. Thus, the pathway to salvation begins with the unmasking of the central illusion, which is synonymous with the release from bondage to the limited self. Merton chooses the words of St. John of the Cross to refer to the next stage in this process of developing self-consciousness. One turns directly to the nothingness within, facing the emptiness without reservations, to discover "the nothing that is all." The word "epiphany" (making manifest) belongs to the description too, for Merton refers to the manifesting of the life of God within. This is synonymous with union with God. It can also be expressed as giving formation to the life of Christ, for Christ is the articulation of God in human terms, both exteriorly and interiorly, both in the world and in one's most inmost self.

Obviously, there are powerful social and political implications. Merton's suggestion in this regard is that the problems of the world cannot be approached on a piece-by-piece basis: first this problem and this plan of action, then this problem and this place of action, then, etc. Instead, the whole structure of human consciousness must change. It is not a matter of discovering remedies and of resolving problems. Rather, it is necessary that men and women come to a radically different understanding of themselves. Problems cannot be solved if the conditions for centering the human being are not present.

Because of his notoriety, the popularity of *The Seven Storey Mountain*, and his influence in the area of monastic reform and the cultivation of personal spirituality, Merton often felt obliged to explain or articulate the style of life he had selected. In a brief essay entitled "As Man to Man," he once described the monk's role in the following way:

I have been summoned to explore a desert area of man's heart in which explanations no longer suffice. . . . An arid rocky dark land of the soul, sometimes illuminated by strange fires which men fear and peopled by spectres which men studiously avoid except in their nightmares. And in this area I have learned that one cannot truly know hope unless he has found out how like despair hope is.[24]

From here the sequence is natural, from despair to hope, from hope to love, from human love to a profession of dependence upon God's love. The affirmation follows: "love is the epiphany of God in our poverty."

The summary identification paragraph reads as follows:

The contemplative is not the one who has fiery visions of the cherubim carrying God on their imagined chariot, but simply the one who has risked his mind in the desert beyond language and beyond ideas where God is encountered in the nakedness of pure trust. . . . The message of hope the contemplative offers is not that you need to find your way through the jungle of language and problems . . . but that whether you understand or not God loves you, lives in you, dwells in you. . . . The contemplative has nothing to tell you except to reassure you and say if you dare to penetrate your own silence and risk sharing that solitude with the lonely other who seeks God through you and with you, then you will truly recover the light and the capacity to understand what is beyond words and beyond explanations because it is too close to be explained: it is the intimate union in the depths of your own heart, of God's spirit and your own secret inmost self, so that you and He are in all truth one spirit.[25]

It is this rekindled spirituality together with the contention that redeemed social structures depend upon altered human consciousness which makes Merton's thought both helpful and attractive. For his approach holds the promise of being able to spark the same sort of transition one finds, say, between the monasticisms of St. Anthony and St. Benedict. The former offered a clear alternative to the relationship to reality which had been condoned in the Graeco-Roman world. The latter understood monasticism to be reconstructive, and not simply a workable alternative. In St. Benedict's view, monasticism was the instrument of transition to a compelling and pervasive new social order. St. Anthony was the originator of the monastic "counterculture" in the Christian West, but his was more critique than composition. With Benedict, as with William Irwin Thompson's response today, after the step has been taken beyond "the edge of history," the monastic alternative became one of the prime means by which the cultural heritage is transmitted, reworked, reconstituted, and redesigned. The Merton of *The Seven Storey Mountain* is more Anthony than Benedict, but the eventual Merton carries the potentiality of being a Benedict, particularly if the new reconstitution of the heritage includes a mixture of things from non-western culture and trans-western religious experience. In Merton something of the nerve and character of the counterculture live on.

NOTES

1. Maurice Merleau-Ponty, "Faith and Good Faith," in *Sense and Non-Sense*, trans. Hubert L. and Patricia Allen Dreyfus (Evanston: Northwestern University Press, 1964), p. 174. In the same essay, Merleau-Ponty added, "The paradox of Christianity and Catholicism is that they are never satisfied with either an interior or an exterior God, but are always *between* one and the other" (p. 177).

2. One of the Camaldolese was quoted this way in an article on "Big Sur Monastery Retreat," *The Gardena Valley News*, December 14, 1972, p. 44.

3. William Irwin Thompson. *At the Edge of History* (New York: Harper and Row). Significantly, Thompson described his journey to the monastery, but relates none of the details of what happened after he arrived.

4. Thomas Merton, "Is the World a Problem," Chapter VIII of *Contemplation in a World of Action* (Garden City: Doubleday and Company, 1973), pp. 158–171.

5. St. Teresa of Avila, *Interior Castle*, trans. and ed. F. Allison Peers (Garden City: Doubleday and Company, 1961).

6. In referring to Søren Kierkegaard, I am thinking specifically of his attempt to create a grammar of the interior life.

7. I have explored these suggestions, in part, in my "Nathan Söderblom: Homo Religiosus?" *Lutheran Quarterly* 12 (1969); pp. 392–396. The occasion for such suggestions is documented

by Bengt Sundkler in his biography of Söderblom, *Nathan Söderblom. His Life and Work* (London: Lutterworth Press, 1968).

8. For an account of Thompson's intentions in founding Lindisfarne, see William Irwin Thompson, "Lindisfarne: A Planetary Community," *The Futurist* 9, No. 1 (1975); pp. 4–8.

9. See Needleman, "The Used Religions," in Jacob Needleman and Dennis Lewis, *Sacred Tradition and Present Need* (New York: Viking Press, 1975). This is the chapter which contains an account of the pilgrimage to which I have made reference. Needleman's other books are *The New Religions* (New York: Doubleday and Company, 1970); and *Religion for a New Generation* (New York: Macmillan Co., 1973), coedited with A. K. Bierman and James A. Gould.

10. I am referring specifically to Merton's final lecture in Bangkok in 1968, on "Marxism and Monastic Perspectives," in which brief but sympathetic treatment is given to Marcuse's views. See Appendix VII of *The Asian Journal of Thomas Merton*, ed. Noami Burton, Brother Patrick Hart, and James Laughlin, consulting editor, Amiya Chakravarty (New York: New Directions Books, 1973), pp. 326–343.

11. Ibid., p. 341.

12. I am basing this observation on the tone of Zaehner's treatments of the interrelationships between the religious traditions of the world, as his viewpoint is presented in such works as *At Sundry Times* (London: Faber and Faber, 1958); *Evolution in Religion: A Study of Sri Aurobindo and Pierre Teilhard de Chardin* (Oxford: Clarendon Press, 1971); and *Matter and Spirit. Their Convergence in Eastern Religions, Marx, and Teilhard de Chardin* (New York: Harper and Row, 1963).

13. Merton, *Contemplation in a World of Action* (New York: Doubleday and Company, 1973), p. 174. Copyright © 1973 by Doubleday & Company; reprinted by permission.

14. The larger passage reads as follows: "Teilhard de Chardin is one witness among many—doubtless the best known—to a whole new conception, a dynamic, immanentist conception of God and the world. God is at work in and through man, perfecting an ongoing Creation. This too is to some extent a matter of creating an acceptable image, a picture which we can grasp, which is not totally alien to our present understanding, and it will doubtless be replaced by other images in later ages." Ibid., p. 175.

15. Ibid., p. 27.

16. Ibid.

17. Ibid., pp. 27–28.

18. Ibid., p. 53.

19. Ibid., p. 54.

20. Merton, *The Seven Storey Mountain* (New York: Harcourt Brace Jovanovich, 1948), p. 135.

21. Merton, "Marxism and Monastic Perspectives," *Asian Journal of Thomas Merton,* p. 335.

22. Ibid., p. 329.

23. Ibid., p. 332.

24. Merton, "As Man to Man," *Cistercian Studies* 4 (1969): 90–94.

25. Ibid.

CHAPTER SEVEN

HOPE'S REVISED CHARTER

I was concerned then with the remembrance of Christ in the form of the hope of his future, and now I am concerned with hope in the form of the remembrance of his death.
— Jürgen Moltmann[1]

It is instructive to view the career of hope theology as a parallel to the interest in the counterculture. To a large extent, the two phenomena can be viewed as allies. Indeed, the theology of hope may be a theologically-sanctionable Christian description of the counterculture. Of course, for counterculture advocates, hope theology didn't go far enough. Its theological sanctions prevented it from being radical enough to pass as a counterculture motif. In this regard, it was more a revised Apollonian than a fully developed Dionysian rendition. This characterization becomes apparent in the well-intended but missed dialogue-exchange between Moltmann and Sam Keen on the subject of play.[2] And, from the other side, some of the hope theologians must have viewed counterculture philosophy as being in danger of passing beyond respectability by virtue of its penchant for destroying the very categories it sought to transform. But, given a host of qualifications, there were many telling similarities between the two developments, even though parties to either side may not have known or recognized the other. For example, the revolution in Christian awareness occurred at about the same time that counterculture advocates were announcing that human consciousness had been altered. Both movements occurred at the edges of "normative culture." Each was manifestly anti-establishment, and both were supremely idealistic. In opposition to the view that reality was determined or pre-fixed, Metz' injunction to keep life moving and free could be translated easily into counterculture language. Both talked of the imminence and immanence of human salvation. And both confessed that there could be no true salvation for any one person unless the conditions of salvation—the very images through which salvation is conceived—were significantly revised and renewed. Both attitudes spawned their own myths and rituals, and, occasionally, such myth-and-ritual sets dramatically overlapped. Significantly, what happened to the counterculture happened also to hope theology. In both cases there was large initial enthusiasm, aligned with espoused shifts in orientation of consciousness, followed by specific political action, resulting in debilitating disappointment, then diffusion.

According to impressive earlier proclamations, the present era was to have been a time of joyful corporate celebration and deep personal fulfillment. This the songs, liturgies, and Sunday's homilies foretold. It should have been the time following a successful, pervasive, nonviolent revolution, or so previous projections had read. It should have been an era formed by the raising of human consciousness, or so many theologians, humanistic psychologists, social planners, ecologists, environmentalists, writers, lyricists, and other analysts and commentators had proposed. It was intended as a new time, where human awareness had plumbed to significant new depths, marked by the bursting forth of fresh possibilities for humanity, with flowers everywhere.

But it wasn't. Or was it? It was? Then why wasn't it?

"It is winter in America, or so it seems," wrote Robert Bellah, in November 1973.[3] Watergate, the War in Vietnam, the lack of confidence in government, inflation, violations of freedom of choice, as well as the general malaise regarding national purpose provided little occasion for festivity, nothing to celebrate, no feeling of accomplishment, no achievement of closure, no anticipation of springtime. If it had dawned at all, the new era had been submerged, perhaps skillfully subverted, due to pessimisms from another source. If it had become present at all, the new consciousness was forced to turn back upon itself. A new era of form, structure, and order had replaced expectations of innovation, freedom, and unburdening. Loisy remarked almost a century ago that Jesus came to preach the kingdom of God, but it wasn't the kingdom that came but the church.[4] Then Loisy added that when the church came it preached Christ. It was a similar phenomenon this time: not the new era, not the new realm of freedom, but something less uncommon, less daring, more cautious, a surrogate for the dynamic reality that was expected.

Deeply disappointed, and somewhat chastened, eschatologs and advocates of the counterculture went underground again, their efforts dissipated, or having become acculturated. The flowers faded. The music turned cold. The homilies turned back to more traditional themes, motivated by a demand for restabilization. And yet the urgency of the new demand was more unsettling than the unsettlement it sought to remedy. It was to have been something different, but this something different—this almost archaic something different—was not expected. It was not the time of ultimate realization, but a season of highs and lows, in uneasy but rapid succession, in perpetual oscillation, the one interchanging with the other, following the recent advent, then demise, of hope. Or, if the previous signs of hope had brought fulfillment, such accomplishments, like the dawning of the apocalypse, seemed more subtle than explosive or self-evident. Sweeping changes had come about, indeed, but they encountered the force of their contraries. Thus, for both the theology of hope and the career of the counterculture, there was large initial enthusiasm, aligned with espoused shifts in orientation of consciousness, followed by specific political action, resulting. in apparent disappointment, debilitation, then diffusion.

But if it is true that hope has seen disappointment, and its earlier optimism has been quelled, it does not necessarily follow that its career is over. At the moment the movement is suffering from overextension. It may have gotten tired, but it isn't finished. The initial band of advocates feels less deceived and exploited than confused. They believed in their goals, and they sensed the large creative strength of their avowals. Perhaps they were naive about strategy. The accomplishments haven't matched expectations. So, following disappointment and confusion came diffusion, and eventually transference. Some of the primary energies became lost in self-reflection, or were redirected toward other interests.

Jürgen Moltmann, the conceptualizer of the theology of hope, addressed this situation in a lecture on apathy which was sponsored by the Center for Ethics and Social Policy in Berkeley in 1974.[5] From the fuller title, "Hope and the Apathetic Person," the audience expected some new recommendations for those advocates of hope who had been ravaged by frustration, disappointment, and unconcern, and had fallen understandably into a state of both religious and ideological indifference. In other words, Moltmann's hearers expected his discourse on apathy to offer regenerative response, renewed encouragement, to those persons who, at one time, had tried to be persistent in hope. One would expect Moltmann to use this occasion to battle the recurrence and prevalence of apathy among Christians in the modern world. In an earlier era, hope was announced as an alternative to despair, and its charge was renewal, not mere restoration. Ten years later the opponent is not despair, but frustration, indifference, and apathy exhibited among those who took renewal as their *raison d'être*. Further, one would expect that apathy would be construed as uncommitment, disengagement, and broken or shattered involvements. These expectations are well founded, and they seem to be encouraged both by the context and by the title of Moltmann's address.

But there are some surprising elements in the address. The true alternative to apathy is not hope, but pathos. And hope lies on the side of pathos rather than on the side of apathy. Ironically, there is a brand of hope which produces apathy, but this is not the hope that derives from "the true origins." Hope-become-apathy results from an overcommitment, to "activity, success, progress, and development." It is not simply that activity, success, progress, and development sometimes goes awry, leaving its devotees weary, frustrated, and confused. Apathy is not only the product of negative success stories. No, Moltmann's contention is more dramatic. In his view, apathy is produced by the confidence that has been placed in reform programs of one sort or another. Apathy is provoked even by programs that succeed. Optimism creates apathy. Programs of action stimulate apathy. The commitment to progress and to human betterment invokes apathy. Apathy is the proper consequence of this mode of being in the world, regardless of the relative strengths of successes and failures. Apathy follows upon commitment to activity, success, progress, and development. And, to make matters worse, political theologies have promoted apathy, perhaps unwittingly. The theology of hope kindled apathy. This is the dramatic element in Moltmann's most recent statement, for, when it first came to light, the theology of hope was recommended in part because of its ability to present itself as a political theology opposed to the political quietism of earlier theological positions.

In the same address, Moltmann went on to observe that political conservatives and political revolutionaries are caught in the same box of apathy. The conservatives rely upon past successes, and resist innovation through their devotion to the past. The revolutionaries are committed to instigating "new and different successes," that is, departures from the past. Their strength derives from present, current, and perpetual innovations. But all of it—both conservative and revolutionary forms of political innovations—derive from the same attitude or disposition. Both testify to a commitment to programs of action in order to facilitate progress, assure human development, and achieve both short- and long-term successes. Referring to the intentions of both conservatives and revolutionaries, Moltmann suggests:

Both stem from the same stock. Theirs is a God of action—the strong God, ever on the side of the stronger battalions, the God who wins battles and leads his own to victory. He is the idol of humankind's success.[6]

He then goes on to speak of an alternative—not only an alternative to this conception of deity, but also an alternative to confidence in political programs. He speaks of "the other, the weaker, the more sensitive side of life"—sounding very much like Dietrich Bonhoeffer's reference to the God "who has been edged out of the world and onto the cross."

The more sensitive side of life is the side of deeper pathos. And this contrast is employed to introduce Moltmann's appreciation for a God who suffers:

Now this God of success and the apathetic individual of action contradict completely that which we find at the core of Christianity—the suffering God and the loving and in-love invulnerable human. The crucified God, conversely, contradicts the God of success and the idol worshippers, the officially optimistic society. The old rugged cross contradicts the old and new triumphal theology which we produce in the churches to keep pace with the transformations of an activist society.[7]

Then come new recommendations: (1) there is no theology of hope which is not first a theology of the cross, thus a theology of suffering and the crucifixion; (2) apathetic existence—produced by zealous commitment to action—must be transformed into an existence of *pathos*. Does this mean that the new theology of hope, one aligned with action rather than theory, has recently gone ascetic? Perhaps this reads in too much, but there are strong tendencies in this direction. The implications follow:

In the sphere of the apathetic God, we become *homo apathetikos*. In the situation of God's pathos, however, we become *homo sympathetikos*.[8]

A much fuller and more detailed treatment of the same theme occurred in Moltmann's most recent book, *The Crucified God*, published in English translation in November 1974. In the introduction to the book, entitled "in explanation of the theme," Moltmann argues that his *theologia crucis* marks no departure from his previous theology of hope. Instead, it is intended as a treatment of the same theme, but from the other side. Anticipating the question about the geneology of his new emphasis upon crucifixion, Moltmann writes:

I may be asked why I have turned from "theology of hope" to the theology of the cross. I have given some reasons for this. But is it in itself a step backwards? "Why," asked Wolf-Dieter Marsch with approval, "has Moltmann come back from the all too strident music of Bloch, step by step to the more subdued *eschatologia crucis*?" For me, however, this is not a step back from the trumpets of Easter to the lamentations of Good Friday. As I intend to show, the theology of the cross is none other than the reverse side of the Christian theology of hope, if the starting point of the latter lies in the resurrection of the *crucified* Christ. As I said in *Theology of Hope*, that theology was itself worked out as an *eschatologia crucis*. This book, then, cannot be regarded as a step back. *Theology of Hope* began with the *resurrection* of the crucified Christ, and I am now turning to look at the *cross* of the risen Christ. I was concerned then with the remembrance of Christ in the form of the *hope* of his future, and now I am concerned with hope in the form of the *remembrance* of his death. The dominant theme then was that of *anticipations* of the future of God in the form of promises and hopes; here it is the understanding of the *incarnation* of that future, by way of the sufferings of Christ, in the world's sufferings.[9]

But in the very next sentence he reveals something of a new departure, at least, a modified departure from previous dependence upon or attachment to Bloch's orientation:

Moving away from Ernst Bloch's philosophy of hope, I now turn to the questions of "negative dialectic" and the "critical theory" of T. W. Adorno and M. Horkheimer, together with the experiences and insights of early dialectical theology and existentialist philosophy. Unless it apprehends the pain of the negative, Christian hope cannot be realistic and liberating.[10]

Then, almost as if the point had not been made forcefully enough, Moltmann repeats:

In no sense does this theology of the cross "go back step by step"; it is intended to make the theology of hope more concrete, and to add the necessary power of resistance to the power of its visions to inspire to action.[11]

It is apparent that we must take Moltmann at his word. His insistence that the *theologia crucis* is not a new interest, or a step backwards, or even a reversal of emphases, implies, then, that hope and crucifixion belong to the same context. Indeed, from the very first, from the time Moltmann was writing about Bonhoeffer—even before that, when Moltmann himself was feeling acutely his plight as a prisoner of war— his thoughts have taken form as *diaspora* writings. Particularly when writing about hope, but also when writing about crucifixion, Moltmann reflects the situation of a stranger or a pilgrim in the land of exile. In the earlier book, the dominant metaphor was that of the exodus. The church was defined as an exodus community, and the schema of Christian salvation was depicted in terms of the realization of the promised land. As we noted, that metaphor articulated well with Bloch's imagery of mankind as a ship over restless waters moving toward a harbor, or a place of identity. In *The Crucified God,* the imagery remains very much the same, although Moltmann gives greater stress in the more recent volume to the pathos and agony of the time of exile and alienation. The same mood was sustained in his in between book, *Theology of Play,* wherein the most substantive treatment of the central theme was offered under the title "How Can One Play in a Strange Land?"[12] In all of these writings, the stress lies on captivity, alienation, exile, oppression, the exploitation of the oppressed, the qualitative distinction between *now* and *what will be,* and on the distortion and deceptions which occurs in one's relationship to reality when *now* and *what will be* are confused.

In *The Crucified God,* the familiar themes are sounded with new force, and the dominant metaphor—the alien in a land of exile—is described in greater depth and in more detail. But in *The Crucified God,* the problem is not just that the pilgrim is still in process, at some distance from his goal. Moltmann is more explicit. The problem is that the context is defined as "godforsakenness." The pilgrim is forced to strive from within a "godforsaken" world. The Christian as alien and exile is obliged to confront pervasive absence of meaning, to which Moltmann refers to as "ossified life" and "absurd life."

The context is still Bonhoeffer's world, the world of the cell, where the prisoner (in exile, as alien) is forced to rely upon the power of One who is powerless in that situation. The pilgrim's God is Bonhoeffer's "God who has been edged out of the world," the God who has been forced to forsake the world. Moltmann accepts Bonhoeffer's paradox that the powerlessness of God in this world, the world of exile and alienation, is also God's power in the world. The crucifixion of God, in short, articulates appropriately with Moltmann's understanding of man's plight and of the means of its clarification.

The exodus context and the imagery of exile and alienation are sustained in Moltmann's depiction of the God who "suffers in his passion for his people." Citing P. Kuhn's work on rabbinic theology, he writes:

. . . the rabbis at the turn of the ages spoke of a number of stages in the self-humiliation of God: in the creation, in the call of Abraham, Isaac and Jacob and the history of Israel, in the exodus and in the exile. Psalm 18.36: "When you humble me you make me great" was understood to mean: "You show me that you are great by your humiliation of yourself." God dwells in heaven and among those who are of a humble and contrite spirit. He is the God of gods and brings justice to widows and orphans. He is lofty and yet looks upon the lowly. So he is present in two opposite ways. God already renounces his honor in the beginning at creation. Like a servant, he carries the torch before Israel into the wilderness. Like a servant, he bears Israel and its sins on his back. He descends into the thornbush, the ark of the covenant and the temple. He meets men in those who are in straits, in the lowly and the small. These *accommodations* of God to the limitations of human history at the same time contain *anticipations* of his future indwelling in his whole creation, when in the end all lands will be full of his glory. He enters not only into the situation of the limited creature, but even into the situation of the guilty and suffering creature. His lamentation and sorrow over Israel in the exile show that God's whole existence with Israel is in suffering.[13]

To illustrate the same point, Moltmann refers to the "shattering expression of the *theologia crucis*," which is found in Elie Wiesel's provocative autobiographical novel, *Night,* in which there is identification between the suffering God and a young boy in Auschwitz "hanging there on the gallows." Then calling suffering "the history in the midst of God himself" and suggesting that the suffering of God can lead us to "the inner mystery of God himself in which God himself confronts us,"[14] he offers the following summary:

The death of Jesus on the cross is the *center* of all Christian theology. It is not the only theme of theology, but it is in effect the entry to its problems and answers on earth. All Christian statements about God, about creation, about sin and death have their focal point in the crucified Christ. All Christian statements about history, about the church, about faith and sanctification, about the future and about hope stem from the crucified Christ.[15]

As the crucifixion is the basis of hope, so is the *pathos* of God responsible for provoking human *sympathy*. The relation of *pathos* and *sympatheia* lead Moltmann back (or ahead) again to a discussion of concrete political action, all of which refers to a process of liberation and unburdening from all forms of oppression and repression in the land of exile and alienation.

The memory of the passion and resurrection of Christ is at the same time both dangerous and liberating. It endangers a church which is adapted to the religious politics of its time and brings it into fellowship with the sufferers of its time.[16]

The rule of the Christ who was crucified for political reasons can only be extended through liberation from forms of rule which make men servile and apathetic and the political religions which give them stability. According to Paul, the perfection of his kingdom of freedom is to bring about the annihilation of all rule, authority and power, which are still unavoidable here, and at the same time to achieve the overcoming of equivalent apathy and alienation.[17]

The following lines from the final paragraph of the book follow almost by implication: "Brotherhood with Christ means the suffering and active participation in the history of this God."[18]

The implication is that there is no straight-line-forward movement into the future, not if the pilgrim is really immersed in a land of exile. In this context, any commitment to programs of action, even to some cryptic ideology of the future, is a concession to fighting the system on the system's terms. Political philosophies and social programs are all deceptive if they are offered as alternatives to or substitutes for the redemptive power of the suffering of God in the world. Such "idols of action and success" can be masqueraded no longer, for hope is rooted in the suffering of God. This is a modification of the conceptual attractiveness of Bloch's philosophy and a return to the prison genre. When the going gets rough, the freedom of the image of the ship traversing restive seas is suddenly transformed into the bondage of the recollection of internment.

When one compares the *Theology of Hope* with *The Crucified God*, and charts the intellectual development through the ten-year cycle, he must wonder. At the beginning of the story, there was tremendous enthusiasm for a new, resourceful, strengthening, and genuinely novel way of conceiving the Christian life. Then years later, there is caution, some reticence regarding possible overcommitment to the new theology, warnings about being exploited by programs of action, hints that social planning is deceptive, testimony that confidence in "plans for the future" possess only a superficial and tenuous base, a profound distrust of a "more sensitive side of life." Moltmann attests that he is looking at one and the same subject from at least two distinct but organically related sides. His most recent work is not intended as a corrective. Neither does it signal a radical break, a lapsing of previous enthusiasms, or a qualification of an earlier commitment. Instead, it is an enriching, deepening probe which belongs in complete continuity with an ongoing self-consistent pattern of development.

Certainly this interpretation must be sustained. Certainly there is an increase in maturity, an enrichening and expansion of the earlier orientation. The difference is that in the newer version, the hope theme no longer stands alone, but is made party to a larger systematic constellation. The linking term is *pathos,* the "deeper sensitivity" that crucifixion lends to hope. Pathos also functions as a conceptual bridge, an instrument of integration, which keeps the relation between past, present, and future intact. In the earlier formulation, it was more hope than pathos, more future than present. God was the God ahead, the God of the future. In the more recent version, God is perceived in the present, where the present is described as "godforsakenness." Here it is more crucifixion than hope, or hope seated in crucifixion, when both together enunciate pathos. When these chief themes are placed in constellation, each one is qualified or defined in relation to the others. The dynamics of systematic reflection regulate the place of any single component. Thus, in moving toward the larger, comprehensive portrayal, the former impact of hope has been de-radicalized, and, to that extent, diminished.

For this reason, one can ponder how Jürgen Moltmann would have been known among us had we encountered him in 1975 and not first in 1965 and then in 1975. If the latter phase of the sequence had been first—even given its religious maturity, its concentration on crucifixion, its testimony to the necessity of suffering and death—would its innovative dimensions have been recognized? Were the latter phase detached from the earlier phase, would there be a theology of hope? Is it enough to say that there is no true theology of hope which is not first of all a theology of the cross? It would seem that the sequence of Moltmann's own discoveries runs in the other direction, and that the force of the recognition ought to be: there can be no true theology of the cross which is not first of all a daring theology of hope. Moltmann's own development is confirming testimony. It was this way too for Karl Barth. And Bonhoeffer's *Letters and Papers from Prison* follows the same course.

Certain forms of Christian piety may welcome the new shift of emphasis. For some Christians, it may even be taken as an occasion for rejoicing. After all, more than a few found Moltmann's initial innovations troublesome. "What about heaven?" the critics used to charge. "How is the kingdom of God an antidote to the need for inner peace or tranquility?" These were questions not fully addressed, not because they weren't important, but because hope's emphases were of another sort "Don't ask a lot of questions about heaven; let's concentrate instead on the characteristics of the kingdom of God!" "Not *credo* right off, not sanctionability, not dogmatic verifiability, but dreams—day-

dreams, fantasies, deep-felt wishes, projections, construc-
tions, creations, and inventive designs!" "Let's not think
orthodoxy first of all, but, rather, be attentive to the compulsions of the creative imagination!" "Not theory, but action
and play." "Let's not be principled by the past (a past that
is now closed to us), but, rather, be open to the immensity
of the future!" This was the response. It involved large
redesigns. Some say the redesigning was too massive.
Many found it impossible to shift this way. Some regarded
the new change as sheer effrontery to the stability of Christian faith. Some deemed the new conversion repugnant.

The same persons may feel some vindication knowing
that significant aspects of that original novelty, alas, have
been tempered by a return to theological fundamentals.
The attitude seems safer now. Earlier excesses have been
brought under firm control, and overstresses have been
brought into balance. From this vantage point, it may even
seem as if the radical theologian has been de-radicalized.
Perhaps his longed-for "travels with Charley" are over, and,
at last, he has come home. We can predict that this is how
Moltmann's recent moves will be interpreted by many, and
that many who found his viewpoint troublesome before will
find it more attractive now.

A more judicious interpretation will see Moltmann's recent moves as an expression of positive and honorable
disengagement. They do not deny the validity of the initial
orientation, while acknowledging that embellishments, alterations, and some redressing of emphases have been made
appropriate by an updated analysis of the contemporary
situation. Moltmann's recent work illustrates that the theology of hope was not intended inflexibly, as though it were
either a final or a complete statement. Thus, disengagement
implies continuity with the recent past through the cultiva-

tion of another point of departure. The prime function of the new or revised point of departure is to transpose the initial orientation into the reflexive mode.

Pathos is accorded these multiple functions in Moltmann's revised outlook. Pathos is both active and passive. It implies involvement, but, fundamentally, through conditioned and cultivated sensitivity. There is hope in pathos, but not hope that is a stranger to sorrow. Pathos is implicit in the confession, "I have been crucified to the world, and the world has been crucified to me." This is the description of the vision in which the imminence of the Kingdom of God is also implicit.

Thus, whatever else *The Crucified God* achieved, it provided support for Moltmann's insistence that theology of hope was neither a school nor a movement, but, in fact, the title of a book. In the decade following, it is as though the author wanted to convince both the school and the movement of the accuracy of this description. So, while becoming richer, better defined, more precise, more conceptually complete, the theology of hope also transcended its own *point vierge*. This is the way it had to be. But in the transition to a deeper seriousness and a nearer maturity there was irretrievable loss of *novum*.

NOTES

1. Jürgen Moltmann, *The Crucified God. The Cross of Christ as the Foundation and Criticism of Christian Theology,* trans. R. A. Wilson and John Bowden from *Der gekreuzigte Gott* (New York: Harper and Row, 1974), p. 5. Used by permission.

2. Cf. Jürgen Moltmann, *Theology of Play,* trans. Reinhard Ulrich, with responses by Robert E. Neale, Sam Keen, and David L. Miller (New York: Harper and Row, 1972). Moltmann acknowledges that the attempted conversation, or dialogue was missed, in the final chapter of the book, when he writes,

". . . the premises from which these replies have been written are not the same as my own—not in the least. We are perhaps not even talking about the same thing. . . . I am at a loss as to what to answer to these three American approaches to play. The authors and I live in the same one world, and yet in completely different inner spaces. A painful realization" (p. 111).

3. Robert N. Bellah, "Reflections on Reality in America," given as the McCall Memorial Lecture, First Congregational Church, Berkeley, California, 1973.

4. Alfred Loisy, *The Birth of the Christian Religion*, trans. L. P. Jacks (London: George Allen and Unwin, 1948).

5. Moltmann, "Hope and the Apathetic Person," lecture given at the Center for Ethics and Social Policy, Graduate Theological Union, Berkeley, California, 1974, which, as far as I know, remains unpublished.

6. Ibid.

7. Ibid.

8. Ibid.

9. Moltmann, *The Crucified God*, pp. 4–5.

10. Ibid., p. 5.

11. Ibid.

12. Moltmann, *Theology of Play*, pp. 1–3.

13. Moltmann, *The Crucified God*, pp. 272-273.

14. Ibid., p. 274.

15. Ibid., p. 204.

16. Ibid., p. 326.

17. Ibid., p. 329.

18. Ibid., p. 338.

CHAPTER EIGHT

MOLTMANN AND MERTON

I have been summoned to explore a desert area of man's heart in which explanations no longer suffice. . . . An arid rocky dark land of the soul, sometimes illuminated by strange fires which men fear and peopled by spectres which men studiously avoid except in their nightmares. And in this area I have learned that one cannot truly know hope unless he has found out how like despair hope is.

—Thomas Merton[1]

The prisoner experienced an inner conversion when he gave up hope of getting home soon, and in his yearning he rediscovered that deeper "hope against hope." Hope made him free to accept, even laugh at the barbed wire, and to discover in his fellow prisoners human beings whose company he enjoyed, with whom he could be happy even in suffering. An American periodical once stated that the theology of hope was born in a prisoner of war camp. Autobiographically speaking, I believe it may have been correct. But the hope that was born there was not that painful, disturbing hope, but rather a deeper, liberating hope which works through love.

—Jürgen Moltmann[2]

The religious scene that was envisioned only a few short years ago is very different now. Time did invade the cathedral. Change did come to challenge permanence. The conception of the religious life in classical, vertical terms was transformed, or turned on its side, through the increasing compulsion of horizontal sensibilities. The former fortresses against time's destructiveness, the veritable bastion's of permanence's reign, were bracketed or jettisoned in favor of an openness to novelty and innovation. The Christian world had gone experimental. Classical baroque had given way to Danish modern. The music of the pipe organ was blended with syncopated guitar. The old assurances—firm, constant, dependable, inveterate, constructed to last and last and last—were challenged by a disposition lighter, sleeker, more delicate, less sure, fanciful, never pompous, deliberately tentative and portable, almost kinetic. Time had invaded the cathedral, and the image of permanence and stationariness had been quelled by the excitement of spontaneity, mobility, flexibility, and enchantment with possibility. The occurrence of the *novum* required that one's relation to the entire world be nuanced by the future tense.

But the future was gained through extensive loss. And eventually, indeed, rather quickly, loss also spelled the relinquishment of recent gains. The future got lost through the very preoccupation with the future. The future became lost shortly after past and present were jettisoned on behalf of the future. Openness to novelty tended to mitigate perception of durability. The urge to revise and reconstruct took valuable energy from the obligation to preserve and refurbish. In redressing our priorities by means of a full modal shift to the future, whose articulation required an alternate sensibility, we were shortsighted and too eagerly and unwarily fundamentalist. We had been to the future, and the future was exciting. But in expecting too much we lost hold of a more catholic vision which could have provided us far more.

"Civilization is a very delicate plant," E. H. Gombrich once wrote to the Editor of the *London Times*, "and we cannot be sure that it will always survive." The same can be said of culture. The same may be said of a religious tradition. It is an intricate and fragile plant. Its survival is not always guaranteed. Unless steps are taken to safeguard it, it can lose its resilience. And then it can quickly degenerate into historical record.

Indeed, as Moltmann's recent work seems to illustrate, the path into the future may require, at least initially, a step away from immediacy and encounter. It may be necessary for us to reach down or back to recover things we have lost sight of before we can find the resourcefulness to take a truer, more significant step into the future. Some of us, for example, were taken with the thought that we had to juxtapose the usual way in which time tenses had been employed in Christian awareness. We had become sold on the idea that it isn't enough to keep past traditions alive in the present. Bloch's, Moltmann's, and Metz's creative suggestions—together with a constellation of the same through the artistry of Corita Kent, the architectural explorations of both Soleri and Moshe Safdie, the speculative, imaginative, and all-encompassing scientific work of Buckminster Fuller, the futurology of Kenneth Boulding, the persistent urging of Alvin Toffler, the combined ecological analysis of René Dubos and Barbara Ward—had persuaded us that it was necessary to give some attention to "the pull of the future." And instead of worrying over the fate of past traditions, we tended to place the traditions on the shelves for awhile, within reach should we have need to engage in historical research, but really out of the way of all potential paths of interference, should we choose to proceed in other directions. Moltmann advised us to treat religious truth experimentally, the way scientists approach scientific truth. Some of us accepted the challenge, and proceeded to regard previous theological formulations according to the analogy of worn out medical theory. It is retained for medical records, or for historical purposes, but it possesses no vital present function. Given to another mode, we tried to devote our energies to a creative, innovative experimental use of present and past resources in order to design an inspiring, livable future. After all, hadn't Johannes Metz even defined the Christian God in terms of "the pressure toward maturity exercised upon men and women who recognize that heaven and hell are real possibilities?" This was the call to the future, and many of us tried to rally to its challenges. Accordingly, some went from a theology of hope to a theology of play. Harvey Cox himself called for a discovery of "the gift of true festivity and celebration, for pure imagination and playful fantasy."

Mankind has paid a frightful price for the present opulence of Western industrial society. Part of the price is exacted daily from the poor nations of the world whose fields and forests garnish our tables while we push their people further into poverty. Part is paid by the plundered poor who dwell within the gates of the rich nations without sharing in the plenty. But part of the price has been paid by affluent Western man himself. While gaining the whole world he has been losing his own soul. He has purchased prosperity at the cost of a staggering impoverishment of the vital elements of his life. These elements are *festivity*—the capacity for genuine revelry and joyous celebration, and *fantasy*—the faculty for envisioning radically alternative life situations.[3]

Then, next, Cox described the remedies built into the intention of his *The Feast of Fools*:

. . . I have changed some of my views in the five years since *The Secular City*, and not all these new insights have been entirely reconciled in my own mind. Politically, for example, I have become considerably more radical and would now place myself somewhere near the right fringe of the New Left. . . . I am hopeful in the long run about man's chances, but I see more clearly than I did five years ago that the changes we need are

much more fundamental than I originally thought and that the
method for achieving them must be much more drastic.

At the same time I have become aware that there is an un-
necessary gap in today's world between the world-changers and
the life-celebrators. One of the reasons why I wrote this book is
because I want to see this gap closed. There is no reason why
those who celebrate life cannot also be committed to fundamental social change. And world-changers need not be joyless
and ascetic.[4]

According to a similar mood, Moltmann was found experi-
menting with the techniques of fantasy and play-acting in
his introductory courses in systematic theology at venerable
old Tübingen University. The theological arena was fast
becoming a Disneyland of sorts, where the goal was not
only personal refreshment but also the creation of and participation in fantasy through great leaps of the imagination.

Others of us, with more forensic, but no less novel,
aesthetic bents, began projecting a theology by design. It
was a catchy phrase, and it marked an integer in the sequence of the theologies of hope and play with which it was
interrelated. The theme "theology by design" delineated a
calculated modal shift. The argument was that theological
affirmations could be conceived in a creative, constructive
manner—or "pro-formatively"—and not simply in response
to situations already well set. The suggestion was that
theologians should be able to take cues from the techniques
of future planning. The necessary modal shift could be
facilitated through acquaintance with transpositional models in architectural theory, city planning, and environmental
design. The working assumption was that some of the skills
and principles of design can be translated into conceptual
methodological insights. To have proceeded in this manner
would have been to initiate a second-stage effort, built upon
the partial transformation of perspective established by the

theology of hope. In short, a theology by design made much sense. In many respects, it continues to make sense. Despite all the worried talk and the less rigorous projections, we simply do not yet possess the future, as we might possess it, because we aren't sure yet what future we want. Valuable time goes by and costs soar skyward as we continue to window-shop. The future may remain inaccessible to us because we approach it in inappropriate ways—that is, according to interests alien to the modal shift. We make untoward demands of the future before we have been properly introduced. Such considerations lend large credence to prospective theological ventures in design.

But in our attempt to invoke a modal shift, we also detected that recent transformations had produced losses as well as gains. And before we had proceeded very far, we learned something important about the dynamics of religious sensitivity: religious consciousness tends to move not by stages, progressively, from insight to insight, lending knowledge to knowledge, and wisdom to knowledge, but, instead, almost in the way that surprises are rendered and puzzles are composed. There are definite unpredictable characteristics to the process. Movements of any sort produce countermotion. The total complexion of the scene changes each time a step in any direction is taken. The entire configuration is altered whenever the perspective is shifted or the standpoint is transposed. What is seen to happen depends upon where one is located. Consciousness of one's location is part of one's discovery. The movements forward-backward, inward-outward, upward-downward, earthward-heavenward, timeward-eternalward, bodyward-spiritward, and contrastingly so forth, are unceasing and kaleidoscopic. Each single movement affects the entire composition. At no two points is the profile the same.

At the beginning of the era, Harvey Cox predicted that the two thinkers whose thought would prove to be most worthy of our interest and study in the next several years were Teilhard de Chardin and Ernst Bloch. In retrospect, it is clear that Cox made two very good choices, and that his judgment in linking these figures together was sound. Both Teilhard and Bloch have been extraordinarily important in the years following. They are also unusually suggestive when taken in combination. And despite the attention their writings have evoked, both hold promise of still larger utility in the future. Through R. C. Zaehner, among others, Teilhard's thought has become influential beyond its revisions of Christian theology according to evolutionist conceptual models. Whether beneficially or not, it has also been employed as a perspective on humanity's entire corporate religious history and destiny. As we have noted, Bloch too, partly because of understandable delays and difficulties in translating his writings into English, has more to say than his readers and hearers have yet fathomed.[5] He was and is a tremendously suggestive and powerful writer and intellectual craftsman. As with William Blake, there is virtually no end to the skill, eloquence, and interpenetrability of his verbal imagery. Each time one encounters Bloch's picture-language, he can come away with a host of insights that hadn't occurred before.

Significantly, both of Cox's choices were process-oriented thinkers. He anticipated the full flowering of the process era, and, particularly, its attainment of widespread acceptability and sanctionability in Christian theological circles. He understood that patterns of thought, like styles of life, would become self-conscious strategies of change. He had identified the two most instrumental figures in that theoretical transformational exchange. And he understood that

Bloch and Teilhard had presented their views in a way which traditional orthodox Christian theology would find attractive and generally inoffensive.

But what if the same question were posed today? "What thinkers or spokesmen or representatives are most worthy of present and immediate-future attention?" A firm answer would be difficult to give. The age of the giants is past, we are told. The Tillichs, the Barths, the Niebuhrs have all departed from the scene. And the younger, promising thinkers have not yet attained the eminence and universality that was characteristic of the theological fathers of a recent yesteryear. Perhaps it is no longer necessary that Christian theology follow that grand systematic pattern. Certainly much good work is going on, and excellent mental power and spiritual talent is being directed toward large, significant issues. But present visions seem so much less grand, and present convictions seem so much less sure. The positive temper of several years ago seems to have given in to deepseated and widespread second-guessing. Previous optimism has succumbed to bewilderment. The prophets and visionaries seem to have become quiescent. We are not always confident about the vectors on which we rely to take our readings on the future. We are no longer sure of the ground on which we stand. Indeed, if there are prophets and visionaries any longer, they seem to be restricted to the nations of minority peoples or the third world. This, in itself, is significant, almost as though the responsibility for the *elan* into the future has been shifted into other hands.

What thinker, spokesperson, or teacher is most worthy of present attention? Certainly one can speculate on a question of this sort, and offer a variety of answers to it. When the query was submitted to church people through a number of leading denominational quarterlies and religious news publications early in 1975, first place was given overwhelmingly to Jürgen Moltmann. When the question is transposed from present to future tense, when it is made the subject of conjecture rather than empirical survey research, the choice may have to be Thomas Merton, for the very reasons mentioned in earlier chapters. Indeed, for reasons strikingly similar, it may very well be that Merton's *Asian Journal* will serve the immediate future in much the same way that Bonhoeffer's *Letters and Papers from Prison* has intrigued and informed the present and the recent past. Both works, neither of which was completed because of the tragic deaths of their authors, include suggestions and embrace insights which are not fully elucidated. In both instances, a design for the future is sketched in, though always only tentatively and partially. And yet the designs are both so fascinating and compelling that one can be sure that large future attention will be given to their fuller disclosure. Whereas Bonhoeffer projected Christian consciousness in transition (the content of which was elucidated in impressive fashion in the theology of hope), Merton gives indication of the restructuring of Christian sensibilities via an encounter with the full force of Asian religious experience. It is because of this background that Merton's articulation of the world of "positive disengagement" is both captivating and persuasive. It is because of the presence of the same background factors that Merton can offer his version of "positive disengagement" as something radically different from an irresponsible departure from an engagement of the world. For Merton, positive disengagement is a necessary prerequisite for engaging the world as a deeper reality. And when the Christian Trappist monk makes this claim, he has the whole of the Asian religious world resonating behind him.

But one cannot develop this distinction until after he has noticed and acknowledged how very much Moltmann can be read like Merton, and Merton like Moltmann. We have already alluded to some of the similarities between them, particularly in their dependence upon the same primary metaphor, the image of the pilgrim in passage, their conscious dependence upon a prison or cell literary genre, the shared conviction regarding the basis of human alienation, the compulsion to treat man as an alien and exile, the deep sense that there are periodic deceptions and illusions in one's relation with what is most immediate, as well as the interpretation of the Christian life in terms of the oscillating tendencies between hope and despair. Certainly such common themes bring these two eloquent spokesmen into significant reciprocity. The political theologian and the hermit agree in many respects in their analyses of the present religious situation.

This fact supports the observation that the same data can be made the basis of either political theology or monasticism. It is conceivable that Moltmann's analysis could be used as the rationale to spur one toward monastic life. After all, if God is truly powerless in this world, what would prevent one from seeking a safe enclosure? Similarly, Merton's analysis, steeped in Marxist influenced interpretations of alienation, provides ample and urgent reasons for seeking effective political involvement. From the same base, the same rationale, the same interpretation, Christian response can be directed both ways. In other words, the monastic alternative need not rely upon a "different reading" of reality than that which informs political theology. It is not impossible, for example, to regard Merton as an effective political reformer, nor is it incomprehensible that the theology of hope would be an elaboration of a contemplative tradition whose origins are in Bonhoeffer's cell. But in suggesting that such exchanges are possible, we need not restrict our examples to Merton and Moltmann. St. Benedict was a monk who was extraordinarily effective both politically and culturally. St. Bernard was a monk whose social, political, and cultural sensitivities led him to help heal a papal schism, organize a Crusade, contest the political ambitions of the papacy, while being the dominant religious force of his time. Just as one can see St. Bernard in both roles, so too is it possible to apply the terms active and contemplative to both Merton and Moltmann. Their dominant dispositions are contrary, but not necessarily antithetical or mutually exclusive.

But there is more to the lesson than the truth that contrariness is not necessarily and forever antithetical. For, it is significant that both Moltmann and Merton firmly believe it necessary that the contrary passions be blended and united. Merton's book, *Contemplation in a World of Action*, dramatizes this interest in achieving a comprehensive, integrated viewpoint. Not only do action and contemplation belong together, in Merton's understanding, but the contemplative life is described as "a certain integrity and fulness of personal development" which is entirely compatible with "creative work," "dedicated love," and "fruitful action." The same fusion is enunciated in the statements of intention which the monks of New Camaldoli publish and distribute, wherein the "true goals" and values of the solitary life are distinguished from all flights (some recognizably neurotic) from Christian responsibility. The monks deplore and decry any use of the hermitage as an occasion or instrument for an "egotistic quest for personal quiet, for spiritual consolations or for moral perfection which would deliberately ignore the obligations of charity and the urgent needs of the Church and of mankind." They acknowledge that the solitary life is "conducive to a very special intimacy with God"—an intimacy which is certainly defensible on every religious or spiritual ground. And yet the purpose of their divine vocation is not simply the realization of such solitary intimacy, but, as the words of the Second Vatican Council put it, service "to the Church and to human society." The solitary life is depicted as being "no more than a means to sanctity," which, "in its more absolute forms [is] justified only for those with a very special call and aptitude." The *vita contemplativa* is a mode of life which always adheres to a larger composition of religious dispositions. It can never be employed as a defense of an unambiguous denial of the world. This interlacing of dispositions is implicit in Merton's autobiographical statement:

I want to make clear that I speak not as the author of *The Seven Storey Mountain,* which seemingly a lot of people have read, but as the author of more recent essays and poems which apparently very few people have read. This is not the official voice of Trappist silence, the monk with his hood up and his back to the camera, brooding over the waters of an artificial lake. This is not the petulant and uncanonizable modern Jerome who never got over the fact that he could give up beer. (I drink beer whenever I can lay my hands on any. I love beer, and, by that very fact, the world.) This is simply the voice of a self-questioning human person who, like all his brothers, struggles to cope with turbulent, mysterious, demanding, exciting, frustrating, confused existence in which almost nothing is really predictable, in which most definitions, explanations and justifications become incredible even before they are uttered, in which people suffer together and are sometimes utterly beautiful, at other times impossibly pathetic.[6]

But the same tendency to recapture what seems to have been negated or underplayed is also present in Moltmann, indeed, in the very transition from *Theology of Hope* to

The Crucified God. Like Merton, Moltmann took specific steps, once a definitive statement was made, to provide for its complement. In this regard Moltmann is correct in reporting that crucifixion is not a theme to which he came by stepping back from hope, but, instead, the cultivation of a deeper sensitivity. In a sense, the radical nature of the initial disposition—for Merton as well as for Moltmann—had to be blunted, modified, qualified, or expanded in order properly to account for the truth of its appositional contrary. After being political theology, Moltmann's theology also became a manner of deep religious inwardness, and Merton's contemplative temper has provoked large and profound social and political responses. Neither Moltmann nor Merton is religiously or theologically simpleminded. Both weave their principal stresses into a larger fabric of aspiration.

The similarities between the two are intensive by virtue of the fact that each is committed to a process-conceptual orientation. In this regard, both positions can be described as theologies of change. This description is more obvious in Moltmann's case than in Merton's because of the dominant "this-worldly," immanentist character of the theology of hope. But process is evident also in Merton's formulations. For example, in seeking to recover transcendence, Merton does not return to the classical, hierarchical, predeterministic scheme, but offers supporting arguments on behalf of Teilhard's dynamic, self-creating, horizontal, process vision. And in trying to fashion an alternative to contemporary social and cultural experience, Merton does not abandon the contemporary commitment toward discovering the meaning of life in dynamic processes. In short, Merton's devotion to transcendence is rooted in immanentist sensibilities. The "counterculture" he seeks to sustain can be understood to keep the vision of the theology of hope alive. Both orientations are sensitive to the plight of the pilgrim, the pilgrim in process. Both are eschatologically grounded and are party to an apocalyptic mode. For both the awareness of the reality of the future is absolutely essential.

The prime difference is that Merton is a mystic and Moltmann is not. Thus, for Merton, there is a constant preoccupation with self-transcendence: the awareness of union with God. While the same experience is no stranger to Moltmann, he cannot give it the same strategic central place. The force of Merton's convictions is directed toward transforming self-consciousness. His goal is an alternate understanding of the significance of the self. That understanding includes a recognition that, in some mysterious sense, the human self and the divine self are a single unity. The same recognition leads to a perception of the ingredients of alienation. In mystical awareness, the reality of God is made manifest, and life's underlying unity is made the subject of a recurrent epiphany. For Moltmann, alienation is overcome only through the realization of the kingdom of God. What Merton attains insightfully, through a perceptual and experiential abolition of distortion, Moltmann makes dependent upon the passage and infusion of time. For Moltmann, the transcendence of alienation is reserved for the world of Not-Yet. Because that world is not yet, present religious sensitivity is governed not by mystical union, but by the awareness of godforsakenness. Merton can talk about the tension inherent in "tasting while still thirsting." Moltmann looks for visible signs that oppression, in concrete social and political terms, is being overcome. In a sense, alienation is mediated for Merton by being properly defined. For Moltmann there is no adequate coming to grips with alienation except through the transforming power of specific historical acts and events.

For this reason the lines from theology of hope onward lead through theology of liberation. Alienation is overcome only through the abolition of oppression, and oppression is overcome only when the power of the oppressor is destroyed or nullified. This takes theology of hope away from those who would use it chiefly to redesign Christian thought patterns, and places it in the service of those who are laboring in the gospel to eliminate the conditions of human oppression. In its liberation-theology translation, the theology of hope gains expression in the third world and among minority peoples. It is here that the suffering of God in the passion drama of the world is being most acutely, dramatically, and momentously acted out. But the same redemptive action is not restricted to the environment of the third world: it is present in any situation in which grace is operative in correcting and transforming the plight of the oppressed. In Moltmann's view, one can always locate alienation in a specific and concrete socio-political context. For this reason, effective antidotes to alienation must occur in the same form.

The lines from Merton onward lead not to liberation in cultural and political terms, but toward inspiring new models and paradigms of self-consciousness. Thus, while the movement beyond the theology of hope to a theology of liberation is sequential, Merton's influence evokes a comprehensive modal shift. Through sensitivity to Asian religious traditions, Merton recognizes that there is another mode of self-knowledge than that which has regulated the western mind, a mode which is implicit in contemplative life but which is more fully and eloquently expressed in Asian monasticism. To put the comparative matter over-simply: the tendency set in motion by Moltmann can be regarded as a necessary extension or elaboration of the starting point, while the Merton influence requires a thorough transposition. A similar large-scale transposition made the theology of hope possible: from vertical to horizontal, hierarchical to projective, static to dynamic, past and present to future, permanence to process, establishment to diaspora, theory to action, nature to history, *et al.* Once effected, the comprehensive transposition was extended, embellished, and applied in a multitude of ways, but the transition from *Theology of Hope* to *The Crucified God* required no additional transposition. Its fashioner depicts the same as a fuller, more balanced enunciation. On the other hand, Merton retains Moltmann's turn to process, while effecting an additional transposition. The transposition was influenced by the religious experience of persons of non-western cultures, and pertains to a restructuring of human consciousness.

This explains in part why followers of hope theology found it possible to transfer their allegiances to contemplative religion. For, at about the time theology of liberation was gaining force, many persons of religious sensitivity had discovered the resources of the Asian world, and in the process came to recognize their own capacities for spiritual awareness. Both dispositions led away from the western world *per se*, liberation theology to the third world, and spirituality to the sacred East. Hence, both points of departure possessed implicit rites of passage and specific forms of disengagement, Merton's contemplative spirituality because it was so ordered, and Moltmann's political theology because it provided a programmatic alternative to establishment mores.

The fact is that the contraries come into play regardless

of the initial focus or dominant stress. The turn from theory to action leads to a renewed sense of the necessity of reflection and contemplation. The engagement with contemplation teaches one that contemplation is also regulated by a binarial dynamism—a dynamism which persuades contemplation that it must reach beyond itself. Even here, where singleness of heart seems to be within reach, the force of contrariness becomes all the more apparent. Earlier we observed that the same binarial pattern had seemed to influence conceptions of the relationship between freedom and authority, life and death, spirit and body, heaven and earth, and permanence and change. Now it appears that even the most deliberate human attempt to become interiorly single is pervaded by omnipresent binarial dependencies. Singleness remains as the worthiest of goals, but it cannot avoid contrariness.

If there is one thing necessary, there are at least two factors to reckon with. The one thing necessary belongs to a context within which two realities are discriminated and affirmed. Or as Mircea Eliade suggests, the religious person wants to affirm that all of life is sacred while recognizing that sacred and profane contrast. The religious person seeks integration and wholeness in a discerning, discriminating way. Moltmann finds the substance of integration in the normative process, and refers the fundamental contrast to distinctions in time tenses. In his view, the contrast will eventually be overcome, but the time or moment of integration is not now. Merton makes integration dependent upon the higher, larger, truer, and surer mystical vision, in contrast to which all lesser alternatives are relegated to the world of deception, distortion, and even illusion. Though both are committed to process, Moltmann administers his interpretation of human alienation horizontally, while Merton's temperament retains a preference for the vertical. Moltmann's singleness vs. contrariness is explained through temporal distinctions between *now* and *not-yet*. The fundamental problem, for Merton, is referred to the distinction between visible and invisible, *apparent* and *real*, conflicted and centered.

Must we make a choice? Can we make a choice? Can we have it both ways? Merleau-Ponty observed that "the ambiguity of Christianity" belongs to the fact that the religion of the Incarnation is revolutionary while the religion of the Father is conservative.[7]

This is why the contemporary era is so full of both fascination and anxiety: no matter what trend or point of departure is dominant, regardless of its primary stress, its expression will evoke the contraries. The this-worldly attitude of one orientation will stimulate an other-worldly response. The stress on the life of the spirit will force a recognition of the worth of the body. The emphasis on corporate salvation will provoke a renewed, updated concern for the fate or state of the individual. Calling attention to the absence of God tends to encourage fresh awareness of God's presence. The truth is that the contraries come into play regardless of the conceptual starting point.

At the same time, without diminishing the reality of the complexities of life, religious sensitivity must find a way to honor Luther's affirmation that, within a world in which obligations and freedoms are alternating currents, there is a *unum necessarium*. Religious sensitivity must find a place of rest, a reservoir of simplicity, the occasion for singleness of heart, even in a multidimensional world. This is the profession of the Sisters of Poor Clare, the Camaldolese hermits, as well as the testimony of the theology of hope. The same theme is being enunciated under the rubric "positive disengagement," and it lies at the heart of Lifton's recommendations regarding the protean style. Where there is religious sensitivity, there is demand for singlehearted fidelity. Such fidelity can risk overcommitment and isolation because it cannot tolerate confliction. It attests that in being scrupulously discriminating, one is not necessarily being negative.

This tends to make *homo religiosus*—of any time and place—a seeker after oneness and a custodian of binariness, both at once. Should the demand for oneness be abandoned, binariness is doomed to perpetual protean oscillation to which no rule of measure or principle of regulation is applicable. Should binariness become dislodged, oneness has no proper place. The goal is to find singleness in a world formed by contrasts. Thus, Merton's phrase "contemplation within a world of action" is not quite accurate when taken as a description of the religious intention: not "contemplation within a world of action," but *singleness* in a world in which both contemplation and action are regarded as necessary alternating currents.

Consequently, having known the force of the contraries, one can hardly be tempted to follow religious teachers who declare that the way into the future is straight-line forward or quick steps inward. The trusted guides into the future are probably those persons of resilience who have catholic appreciations for the past, and who recognize that the lines from past to present to future are always multiple and, if you will, odd-job. The future, like the past and present, promises to be characterized by the same profound give-and-take within binarial sets of order. To take one or another of these as though it were the exclusively correct point of orientation is to fail to perceive the presence of alternating currents.

Throughout the preceeding chapters, we have sought to chronicle the binarial action—indeed, the binarial reversals— by which contemporary religious dispositions appear to have been regulated. We have suggested that the past decade has been a time within which dramatic binarial alterations and alternations have occurred. We have not tried to account for these reversals. We have simply noted that they have occurred swiftly, sometimes shockingly and abruptly. We have proposed that these occurrences testify to the protean-like makeup of contemporary religious consciousness. We have also argued that the occurrence of binarial alternation, in recurrent form, reveals something important about the vitality, resourcefulness, and structure of religious sensitivity. Such sensitivity discloses itself as being enormously pliable, and yet it also exhibits a dogged intention to establish singleness of mind, heart, and purpose.

Regarding the nature of contemporary religious trends, our conclusion is that religious aspirations will always be expressed dynamically, sequentially, and in perpetual process of formation. The reason is that there are simultaneous and coextensive dimensions to the religious plane, but they can only be depicted one at a time. Singleness within a binarial context: since it can never be gathered symmetrically, it is perpetually catalytic. The beat must go on and on and on, as the kalaideoscope of expressions seeks new formation, teases out new designs, modulates new sounds according to rhythms of older songs, fashions new melodies through old harmonies transposed into new keys. On and on and on and on—as long as it is appropriate to treat religious aspirations according to the dynamics of conceptual integration.

Are there two religions of Christianity? It certainly seems that way since contrariness forms the working context. And yet the genius of the religion is that both dispositions, interacting contrarily, are necessary to the definitive composition. There were two roads, it seems, the high road and the low road, and both led to Scotland. In the new, updated orchestrated scheme of things, it is not hope against a diametrical opposite, but hope against hope. And the strongest compulsion is against letting either side go.

NOTES

1. Thomas Merton, "As Man to Man," *Cistercian Studies* 4 (1969): 90.

2. Jürgen Moltmann, "Foreword" to M. Douglas Meeks, *Origins of the Theology of Hope* (Philadelphia: Fortress Press, 1974).

3. Harvey Cox, *The Feast of Fools: A Theological Essay on Festivity and Fantasy* (Cambridge: Harvard University Press, 1969), p. 6.

4. *Ibid.*, p. x.

5. A doctoral candidate in religious studies in the University of California, Santa Barbara, Ms. Claire Arneson, is preparing a dissertation under my guidance on "The Concept of Space in the Philosophy of Ernst Bloch and in German Expressionism." One of the finest pieces on Ernst Bloch of which I am aware is the doctoral dissertation written by Tom West which was submitted to the faculty of the Graduate Theological Union in Berkeley in the spring of 1975.

6. Merton, *Contemplation in a World of Action* (New York: Doubleday and Company, 1973), p. 160.

7. Maurice Merleau-Ponty, "Faith and Good Faith," in *Sense and Non-Sense*, trans. Hubert L. and Patricia Allen Dreyfus (Evanston: Northwestern University Press, 1964), p. 177.